SAGE LINE 50 v8

in easy steps

GILLIAN GILERT

COMPUTER STEP

In easy steps is an imprint of Computer Step
Southfield Road . Southam
Warwickshire CV47 OFB . England

http://www.ineasysteps.com

Notice of Liability

Every effort has been made to ensure that this book contains accurate and current information. However, Computer Step and the author shall not be liable for any loss or damage suffered by readers as a result of any information contained herein.

Trademarks

Microsoft® and Windows® are registered trademarks of Microsoft Corporation. Sage Line 50®, Accountant®, Accountant Plus® and Financial Controller® are all registered trademarks of The Sage Group Plc. All other trademarks are acknowledged as belonging to their respective companies.

Printed and bound in the United Kingdom

ISBN 1-84078-201-3

Contents

The Bank   57

5

Products   73

6

Invoices   87

7

Getting Started

This chapter takes you through the stages of preparing the new Sage Line 50 version 8 for use. It explains initial procedures for setting up the various defaults required by the program.

Covers

Chapter One

Introduction

This book covers Sage Line 50 Accountant, Accountant plus and Financial Controller.

All businesses need to keep accurate records of their accounts, but even with a computer program, if the information is not entered correctly, then the accounts could still be wrong. After all, it's easy to blame the computer!

Working through Sage Line 50 version 8 in easy steps

Accuracy reduces errors and prevents costly mistakes.

This book explains in simple, easy stages how to perform the main tasks required for keeping computerised business accounts. The following chapters show how to:

- Set defaults and Company preferences.

- Create customer & supplier records and set up price lists.

Make use of the demo data provided with Line 50 to fully familiarise yourself with the program before getting started. To do this simply click File, Open from the main menu and select Open Demo Data.

- Set up opening balances, maintain Bank accounts.

- Maintain the Nominal Ledger and run an audit trail.

- Generate sales orders and control stock.

- Print invoices, credit notes and statements.

- Produce history and financial reports.

'Preparing to start' checklist

Before getting started with Sage Line 50 version 8 work through the checklist below.

Some things, once entered, cannot be easily changed. Therefore, make sure you have all the relevant information to hand before using Sage Line 50 for the first time.

- Check the start date of your company's financial year.

- Check with an accountant which VAT scheme is used.

- Draw up a list of defaults to use.

- Decide on users and passwords.

With Line 50 version 8 it is possible to change the Financial Year start date after you have already commenced using the program.

- Backup the data if updating Sage.

- Have customer, supplier and bank details to hand.

- Product details, recommend a stock take.

- A list of all opening balances.

Starting Sage Line 50

Alternatively, if a shortcut has been set up on the Windows desktop, you can open Sage Line 50 by double-clicking on the shortcut icon:

Remember that your reporting will not be accurate until all your opening balances have been entered. Ask your accountant for these, if possible before you start using Line 50.

With Sage Line 50 version 8 you can now create multiple delivery addresses so that you can have goods delivered to a number of customer sites whilst specifying a different invoice address.

If Sage Line 50 has been installed for the first time the installation wizard will place it in a folder called Line 50. If you are upgrading from Sage Sterling, Line 50 will be placed in the original SFW folder.

Turn on your computer and wait for the Windows Desktop to appear. To start Sage Line 50 do the following:

1 Click on Start.

2 Point to Programs – a selection appears.

3 Point to Sage.

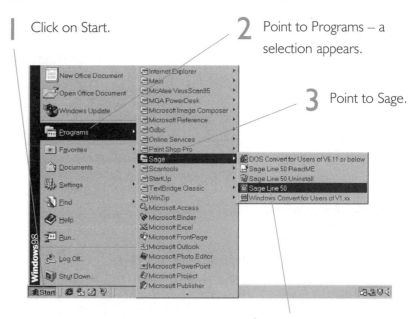

4 Click on Sage Line 50.

The Sage Line 50 desktop appears:

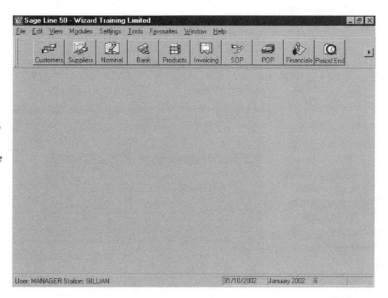

Settings

The Sage Line 50 version 8 CD includes two additional programs, Sage Informer and Sage Forecasting to help you access key financial information and forecast for the future.

Before Sage Line 50 can be used there are a number of settings and defaults that need to be entered. The rest of this chapter shows how to do this. When required, select the appropriate settings option from the following list:

| Click on Settings on the Menu bar.

A quick method of accessing an option from the Menu bar is to hold down the Alt key and press the underlined letter of the function required (i.e., Alt+i pulls down the Settings menu).

2 Click on the option required.

Using Passwords

The Data Protection Act requires that any system containing confidential information, i.e., financial details etc., should be protected against unauthorised access. Sage Line 50 uses a password to achieve this. Once you set a password, Sage Line 50 always prompts you for it at startup.

Click Help on the Sage Line 50 menu bar, then Shortcut Keys, to bring up a diagram of the available shortcuts. Click on the diagram to close it.

As with any password, you should never write it down if it can be avoided. Therefore, try to choose a password that is both easy for you to remember but difficult for someone else to discover. You can decrease the chance of somebody accidentally finding out your password by using a mixture of letters and numbers instead of an actual word.

| From the Settings menu click on Change Password.

Try to avoid using obvious things like a name, phone number or car registration as a password. These are too easy to guess.

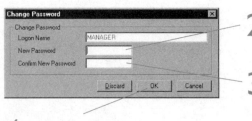

2 Type your password here.

3 Repeat the password here for confirmation.

4 Click OK to save password.

Company Preferences

When you ran Sage Line 50 for the first time the Easy Startup Wizard asked for your Company details. Alternatively, after selecting Company Preferences from the settings options, you can enter these details as follows:

Use the Tab key instead of your mouse to move onto the next line or box.

With Line 50 version 8 you can now enter an alternative address for deliveries by clicking on the Delivery Addresses button.

To have Line 50 print your company details on your stationery, select the Parameters tab and tick the appropriate box in the Printing section.

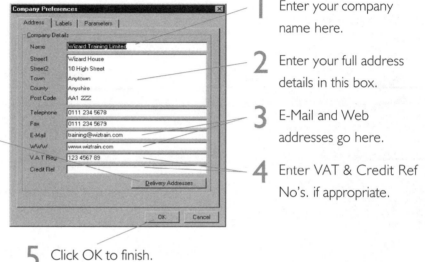

1 Enter your company name here.

2 Enter your full address details in this box.

3 E-Mail and Web addresses go here.

4 Enter VAT & Credit Ref No's. if appropriate.

5 Click OK to finish.

Departments, Product and Fixed Asset Categories

For analysis purposes, you can assign transactions to different departments and divide products and fixed assets into different categories. To set up each of these:

You can assign your transactions to up to 999 different departments and divide Products into 999 different categories. Sage Line 50 also lets you divide Fixed Assets into 100 different categories for analysis & reporting purposes.

1 Click on the required settings option & select the first blank entry.

2 Click Edit to bring up the Edit box.

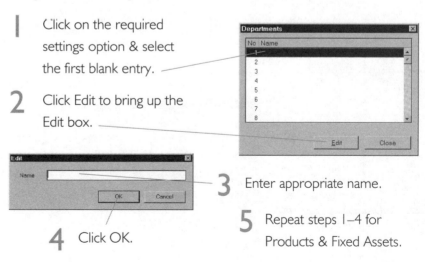

3 Enter appropriate name.

4 Click OK.

5 Repeat steps 1–4 for Products & Fixed Assets.

It is important to use the correct VAT codes. If unsure of current UK or EU VAT Tax rates then contact Customs & Excise.

Use the sage.com button from the toolbar to quickly access up-to-date Customs & Excise and Inland Revenue information via the Internet.

You can specify up to 100 VAT rates, each one identified by a code from T0 to T99. You can then select the rates that are to be included in the VAT Return calculations and which relate to EC transactions.

T1 is the standard VAT rate code.

Sage Line 50 uses T9 as the default tax code for all the routines that are non-vatable, e.g. journal entries and error corrections.

Setting up & checking Tax Codes

Sage Line 50 already has the standard UK and EC VAT Rates set for you together with the code T1 (standard rate – currently 17.5%) set as the default tax code. Here is a list of the codes automatically set up during installation:

T0 – zero rated transactions

T1 – standard rate

T2 – exempt transactions

T4 – sales to customers in EC★

T7 – zero rated purchases from suppliers in EC★

T8 – standard rated purchases from suppliers in EC★

T9 – transactions not involving VAT

(★ *Outside the UK*)

There are 100 VAT codes available in Sage Line 50. To enter or change VAT tax rates:

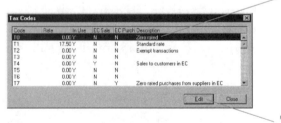

1 From Settings on the menu bar, click Tax Codes, then select the required code.

2 Click Edit.

3 Enter percentage rate.

4 Click here if VAT rate is for an EC Code.

5 Select an EC Purchases & Sales link if appropriate.

6 Enter a Description here.

7 Click OK, then Close.

...cont'd

With early versions of Sage Line 50, once transactions have been posted, the Financial Year cannot be changed. However, you can now change or extend the Financial Year at any time with Sage Line 50 version 8.

Always refer to Sage Help for additional information about changing or extending your financial year.

Use the improved reporting with version 8 to quickly and easily access and analyse your accounting data.

Account Status is a useful feature recently added to Sage Line 50. Use this facility to mark accounts which are bad debts or have exceeded their credit limit, and for placing orders on hold if necessary, etc. If you then raise an invoice, for example, against an account which is a bad debt, Line 50 will issue an on-screen warning.

Financial Year

The start of the financial year is entered during the installation of Sage Line 50 or before entering any transactions:

1 From Settings on the menu bar click on Financial Year then select the first month of your year from the list.

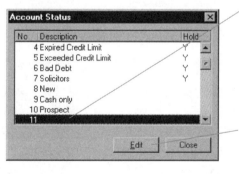

2 Enter the year if not correct.

3 Click OK.

Account Status

A handy feature within Sage Line 50 is that you can assign an account status to each of your accounts. You can add an account status at any time to the ten already set up:

1 Click on Account status from the Settings options then highlight the next available blank status line.

2 Click Edit.

3 Enter Status Name here.

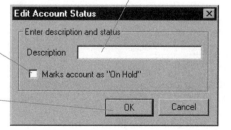

4 Click here if you want this status to place accounts 'on hold'.

5 Click OK to save this new status, then Close.

Currency & the Euro

Initially Sage Line 50 is already set up with the currencies of the EC countries, but not the exchange rates. These details can be edited or other countries set up as required:

Simply press F5 to access the Euro Calculator in any numeric field that displays a calculator button.

1 Click on Settings, Currency and highlight the currency you want to edit or select the first available blank record to enter a new currency.

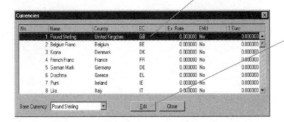

2 Click Edit to bring up the Edit Currency box.

3 Enter the name of the Currency.

The calculator can be used to either view an amount converted from Sterling to a Euro/Foreign Currency or to convert a Euro/Foreign Currency amount to Sterling.

4 Enter the Country here.

5 The EC Member code goes here.

6 Enter the Currency exchange rate.

Exchange rates change frequently, so make sure you have the latest rates entered before recording a foreign currency transaction. Up to date rates are available from a number of sources, including the Internet.

7 Select this box if country is a member of the EMU.

8 Enter the Euro conversion rate here.

9 Click OK, then Close the Currencies box.

Customer & Supplier Defaults

When creating a new customer or supplier, details about credit limit, terms, discount etc. are needed. Customer and Supplier records are fully discussed in Chapters Two & Three respectively but before this, however, defaults need setting up.

For customers, default nominal codes (N/C) start at 4000.

1 Select Customer Defaults from the Settings options.

2 Select this Tab to enter the defaults for your customer records.

From Sage Line 50 version 8, a customer can be a member of a price list.

However, as a customer can only belong to one price list, if you want to change the list that the selected customer belongs to, select the price list you require from the drop-down list. Note that on each price list, additional discounts can still be applied.

3 Click on the relevant Tabs to enter Statements, Ageing Balance and Discount defaults.

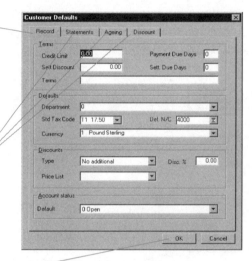

4 Click OK to save Customer Defaults.

5 Select Supplier Defaults from the Settings options.

6 Enter relevant Supplier Defaults here.

Default nominal codes for suppliers start at 5000.

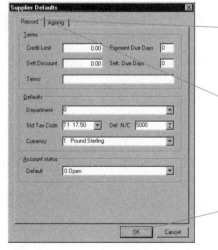

7 Select this Tab to enter Aged Balances Period, specifying calendar months or days.

8 Click OK to save Supplier Defaults.

Product Defaults

Defaults also need to be set up for Products:

1 Select Product Defaults from the Settings options.

 You can use the Finder button on the right of the Nominal Code box to speed up entry.

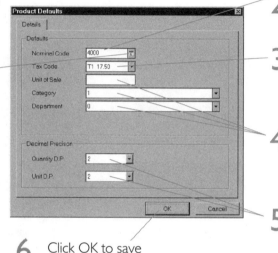

2 Enter the Nominal account code here.

3 Allocate the correct Tax Code for the Product.

 The Finder button is also a quick way of creating a new Nominal Code.

4 Complete the rest of the defaults as necessary.

5 Enter the Decimal Point placing for the product.

 Sage Line 50 allows you to have up to 999 different Product Categories.

6 Click OK to save this information.

Control Accounts

Sage Line 50 uses Control Accounts to make automatic double-entry postings to the ledger.

1 To view or edit these Nominal Codes select Control Accounts from the Settings options.

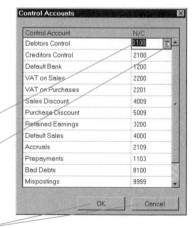

 Unless you have created your own Chart of Accounts, the Control accounts should never need changing.

2 To change a Control account click on the nominal code and type the new code or use the Finder button.

3 Click OK to save and close or Cancel to abandon changes.

Finance Rates

Finance rates need to be set up before any credit charges can be applied to your customers.

When a Finance Charge Rate is applied to a transaction, the first rate charged will be applied monthly until the invoice is paid.

1 Click on the Finance Rates option from the Settings menu to bring up the Finance Charge Rates box.

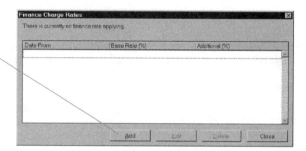

2 Click on Add to enter a new finance rate charge.

You must first have set up your finance rates and the date from which they are to be applied before you can use the Charges option on the Customer toolbar.

3 Enter the date the charge is to be applied from.

4 Enter the Base Rate as a percentage here.

Use the Delete button on the Finance Charge Rates window to remove any unwanted charges.

5 Enter an additional charge here if applicable.

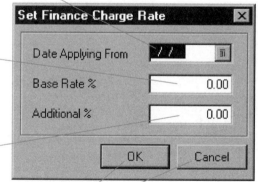

6 Click OK to save new finance rate or Cancel to return to the Finance Charge Rates box.

7 Click Close to finish.

The Sage Line 50 Toolbar

 If any of the Toolbar options do not appear onscreen, click on the arrow button on the left or right of the Toolbar to display them.

From the toolbar the user selects an accounting option by clicking on the relevant button. Alternatively, the required function can be selected from the Modules option on the Menu bar.

 Opens the Customer (sales) Ledger.

 Opens the Supplier (purchase) Ledger.

 To make the buttons more distinct, select Tools, then Options from the menu bar, then check the Show Button Frames box.

 Opens the Nominal Ledger.

 To access the Bank, Credit Cards and Petty Cash accounts.

 Opens the Product Records and Stock accounts.

 To generate Invoices, Credits and related reports.

 To generate Sales Order Processing and reports.

 Opens the Purchase Order Processing window.

 For quick access to the Sage Web site, Customs and Excise or Inland Revenue information just click on the Sage.com button.

Your computer must be Internet-ready (connected to a modem, etc.) to be able to make use of the Internet Browser facilities.

 To access Financial functions (i.e., Profit & Loss, Audit Trail, Trial Balance, VAT).

 Brings up the Period End options.

 Opens the Report Designer window.

 Opens the Sage Line 50 Task Manager window.

 Runs the Internet Browser.

 Brings up a menu of Help options.

The Customer Ledger

In this chapter you will learn how to use the Customer (Sales) Ledger to maintain customer records and create new ones as well as entering credit notes and invoices. You will also be shown how to view transaction activity and set up a customer price list, as well as produce an overdue payments letter, and will learn how to apply credit charges and to mark an invoice as disputed.

Covers

Chapter Two

The Importance of Keeping a Financial System

It is essential for all businesses to have a system to record and monitor their business and financial transactions. This information needs to be accurately recorded and kept up to date if it is to present a true financial position.

Such a system will involve the recording of transactions using the traditional method of bookkeeping or advanced accounting procedures, where financial reports (i.e., profit & loss statements and balance sheet, etc.) can be produced.

These reports provide Management with information on sales, purchases, turnover, expenses, debtors and creditors, assets and liabilities, and more importantly, if the business has made a profit.

The Inland Revenue and HM Customs & Excise (if VAT registered) will also need accurate accounts, which must conform to general bookkeeping and accounting procedures.

This information is also of importance to your Bank Manager, especially if there is a need to borrow money to ease cash flow problems or help set up a new business venture. Likewise, potential investors in your business may first want to see the true financial position of your accounts before making a decision.

Computerised systems have now removed the majority of time consuming and repetitive tasks of manual accounting. Businesses can check their financial status on a daily basis, or over a designated period of time. This valuable information will aid important decision making and business planning and is crucial for forecasting whether a business will succeed or fail.

Sage Line 50 makes keeping computerised accounts easy. Many of the report templates needed are provided with the package, so producing accurate business reports is a simple matter, provided, of course, that all information has been entered correctly. The following chapters guide you through the processes involved in keeping accurate and up to date financial accounts for your business.

The Customers Toolbar

The Customers toolbar provides features for creating customer records and viewing transaction activity, producing invoices and credit notes, marking invoices as disputed and applying credit charges. Customer Statements are produced here, plus letters and a range of reports. With version 8 you can also generate price lists.

New	Creates a new Customer Account.
Record	Opens a Customer Record.
Price List	To set up a Customer Price List.
Activity	Opens Customer Activity.
Aged	Opens Customer Aged Balances.
Invoice	Opens the Batch Customer Invoices window.
Credit	Opens the Batch Customer Credits window.
Dispute	Opens the Disputed Items window.
Charges	Opens the Credit Charges window.
Phone	To automatically Dial a Customer.
Labels	To print Customer Labels.
Letters	To print Standard Letters to Customers.
Statement	To print Customer Statements.
Reports	To run Customer Reports.

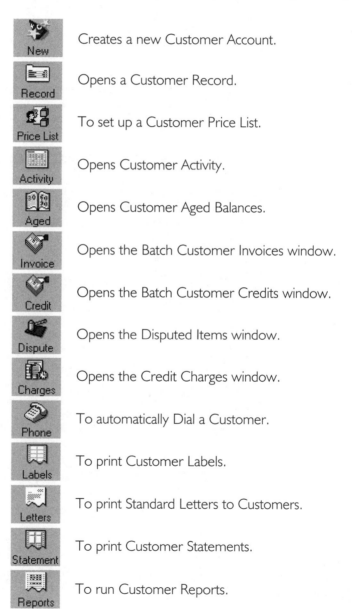

Creating Customer Records

Use the New wizard for simple step by step instructions for entering a new customer record.

Always start by entering the Account Code first. Each customer is given a unique A/C code of up to 8 characters. Use the finder button to locate existing codes.

Sage Line 50 version 8 allows you to record multiple delivery addresses and associated contact details for your customers. Click on the Delivery Addresses button to bring up the display window, from where you can Add, Edit or Delete addresses.

Before you enter an Opening Balance you must have first saved the new customer details.

The method of entering opening balances is different for Standard VAT and VAT Cash Accounting. Use F1 help key to check.

Within this window, a customer record can be added, edited or deleted. You can also record agreed credit terms and even log any contact you have with a customer, such as telephone calls and who you spoke to.

1 Select Customers from the Sage Line 50 toolbar, then click on Record to bring up the Customer Record window.

2 Use Details to store customer name, address and contact information.

3 Use the O/B button to enter an Opening Balance where required.

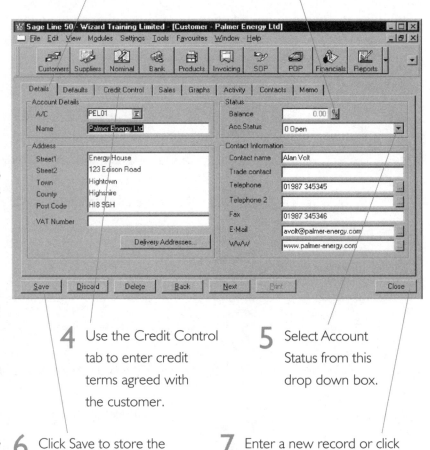

4 Use the Credit Control tab to enter credit terms agreed with the customer.

5 Select Account Status from this drop down box.

6 Click Save to store the Customer Record.

7 Enter a new record or click Close to finish.

Use Activity to quickly view a customer's outstanding balance, Aged Debts etc.

Viewing transactions

Once customer activity has taken place, Sage Line 50 offers you a variety of options for checking customer transaction details:

- View customer invoices, receipts, credit notes and balances on a monthly basis, as a graph or table.

- Use the Activity option to see a breakdown of each customer's transactions.

- View or print the Customer's aged balances.

Note that the following codes identify the transaction type:

SI = Sales Invoice

SR = Sales Receipt

SC = Sales Credit Note

SD = Sales Discount

SA = Sales Receipt on Account

1 Click on the Activity tab in the Customer Record window.

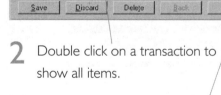

Use the Tidy List button to clear all transaction sub-items from view.

2 Double click on a transaction to show all items.

3 Click on the arrows to scroll through all the transactions.

To view this screen from the Customers window, select the customer required and then click on the Activity button.

4 Click on Range to select another date range or range of transactions, then click OK.

5 Select Close to return to Customer window.

Price List

Where a selected customer is already on another price list, Line 50 asks if you want to transfer this customer to the new list. Click Yes to transfer the customer to the new list or Yes to All to transfer all customers already on another list to the new list.

From version 7, different price lists can be set up and customers allocated to the price list of your choice. For each Price List products can be added and different prices set up accordingly. For example, you can create custom lists for Trade, Retail, Summer or Winter Sales and Special Offers.

To create a new Price List do the following:

1 From the Customers toolbar click on the Price List button to bring up the Price Lists box.

You can also Add or Edit a price list from the Products toolbar.

2 Click Next to open the New Price List window.

3 Enter Reference and Name here.

To Edit or Delete a price list or product from a price list, just select the item and click on the appropriate Edit or Remove/Delete button.

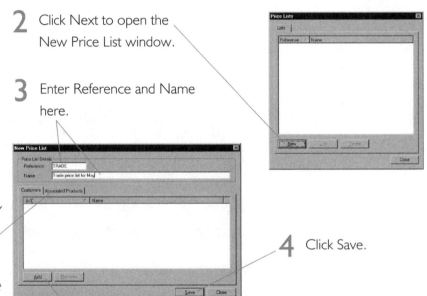

4 Click Save.

To add products to a price list, select the Associated Products tab and follow steps 5–8 as necessary, this time selecting products instead of customers.

5 Click Add to bring up the Add Customers Box.

To add more than one customer at a time to your list, simply hold down the Control key and click on your selection during Step 6.

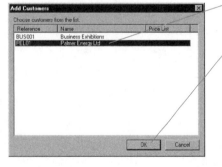

6 Select Customer.

7 Click OK.

8 Click Save, then Close and Close again to return to the Customers window.

Batch Customer Invoice

If you know the first character of the customer A/C, enter it and choose the Finder button to automatically bring up the first code beginning with this character.

Invoices are important business transaction documents and record detailed information about the goods or services supplied to the customer. Briefly, these details include the invoice number, name and address of the customer, date of sale, details of goods and or services supplied, details of discount, total amount of money due and terms of trade.

There are different types of invoices for the task you are carrying out and Chapter Seven shows you how to create a product or a service invoice, as well as automatically creating an invoice from a sales order. However, any invoices produced manually (Batch Invoices) and sent to customers need recording. No printout is produced.

Where you only know the gross value of an invoice, enter it in the Net box and use the Calc. Net button to work out the correct Net value and VAT due.

To record a batch customer invoice do the following:

1 Choose Invoice from the Customers toolbar.

2 Enter the customer Account Code or use the finder button to display a list of codes.

3 Change invoice date if different from current system date.

When you only have a Gross value, simply enter it in the Net box and press the F9 Key to let Line 50 convert it into Net and VAT values for you.

4 Enter the Invoice Number here and a Ref. Number, as required

5 Change Nominal Code or Department if different from defaults.

6 Enter Net value of invoice here.

For a list of useful data entry Shortcut Keys consult the Handy Reference at the start of this book.

7 Click Save to update the nominal ledger and customer details (details posted), then Close.

Always check that the correct Tax Code is used. See page 12.

Batch Customer Credit Note

A credit note is used, for example, where an error is made and a customer has been overcharged on an invoice. Sometimes, damaged goods are returned and so a credit note is issued showing the amount due to the customer.

Like batch invoicing, credit notes processed manually need entering. To record batch credit notes:

To check the credit note has been posted, make a note of the balance for the appropriate customer in the Customers window before entering the credit note, then check that the balance has reduced by the correct amount after performing Step 6.

1 Click Credit from the Customers toolbar to bring up the Batch Customer Credits window.

2 Enter the customer Account Code.

3 The screen displays the defaults for the nominal account code posting, VAT rate to be applied & department.

When looking at Customer activity, the transaction type (Tp) code SC indicates a Sales Credit Note.

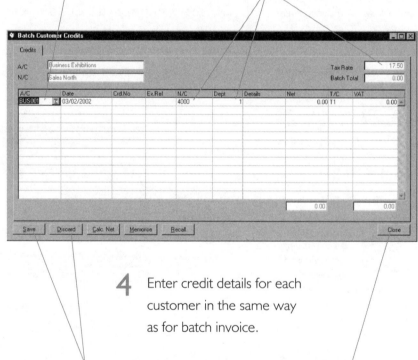

If you need a printout of a credit, generate a product or service credit note from Invoicing on the Sage Line 50 toolbar and the details will be recorded automatically.

4 Enter credit details for each customer in the same way as for batch invoice.

5 Check all values are correct & click Save to post the details or Discard to start again.

6 Click Close to return to the Customers window.

Debtors Analysis

Use Customer Defaults from the Settings menu to change the age of the debt between calendar months and period of days.

To identify debtors and monitor cashflow, customers' outstanding balances and transactions need to be regularly checked. These transactions are grouped by the age of the debt, either on calendar months or based on a period of days, e.g. 30, 60 and 90 days etc. Debt chasing letters can be issued if required. Some businesses may use this information to calculate interest charges for late payment.

To help you keep track of your Aged Debtors, Sage Line 50 provides a large selection of Aged Debtors Analysis details in the reports section for printing out.

1 From the Customers window select the required customer.

2 Click Aged to bring up the Aged Balances Date Defaults box.

3 Enter the date to be used for calculating the aged balances.

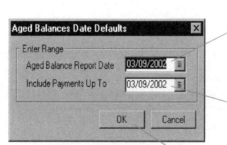

4 To include payments only up to a particular date, enter that date here.

When viewing aged balances in graphical format use the Options facility to select what information you wish to view in the graph.

6 To see the aged balances in graphical format use the Graph tab.

5 Click OK to bring up the Aged Balances window.

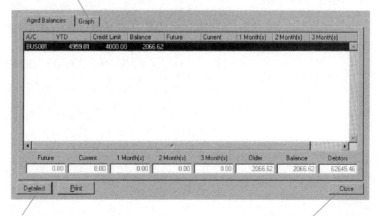

When you select the customers you require in the Customers window, check that the dates entered in the Aged Balance Report Date and the Include Payments Up To boxes cover those selected customers.

7 For a transaction breakdown click on Detailed.

8 Click Close to return.

Credit Charges

Interest rates applied to credit charges are set using the Finance Rates option from the Settings menu.

A payment which is 30 days overdue is regarded, by default, as late. If you need to change payment terms, do the following:

1 From the Sage Line 50 toolbar choose the Customers button.

2 Highlight the appropriate customer or customers, then click the Record button.

Use the Memo box to keep notes on a credit agreement negotiated with the selected customer.

3 Click on the Credit Control tab to bring up the Credit Control details box.

4 Enter new details in Pay Due Days.

From November 1998 credit charges can be applied for customers whose payments are overdue. To apply this, from the Customers window click Charges to run the Credit Charges Wizard, then follow the instructions.

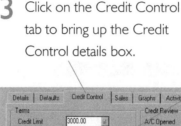

| Details | Defaults | Credit Control | Sales | Graphs | Activity | Contacts | Memo |

Terms
- Credit Limit: 3000.00
- Sett. Due Days: 15
- Sett. Discount: 2.50
- Pay Due Days: 30
- Terms: 30 days
- Credit Ref.: TS3809
- Bureau:

Credit Review
- A/C Opened: 01/03/1999
- Last Credit Review: 02/02/2001
- Next Credit Review: 02/08/2001
- Application Date: 28/02/1999
- Date Received: 01/03/1999

Memo:
A/C open date:
Trade references checked out ok.
Passed credit check review account 3-12 months

First Review
Satisfactory account

Restrictions
- ☑ Can charge credit ☐ Restrict mailing
- ☑ Terms agreed ☑ Account On Hold

Save Discard Delete Back Next Print Close

5 Apply account restrictions here if desired, such as placing account on hold, allowing credit to be charged etc.

Before you can use the Wizard, finance rates must have first been set up.

6 Change any of the other terms as required, then click Save.

7 Click Close to return to the Customers window, then Close again.

Disputed Invoices

For a quick list of all your invoices that are marked as disputed, print out the Customer Invoice Disputes report from the Customers, Reports window.

There may be times when an invoice is questioned by the customer, so until an agreement is made the invoice can be marked as disputed. This option also applies to any invoices not fully paid. Once the problem is resolved, you can remove the disputed flag (indicator). To mark an invoice as disputed:

1 Click on the Dispute button in the Customers window to bring up the Disputed Items window.

Don't forget that you can always use the Finder button to locate the A/C from a drop-down list.

2 Enter the Customer Account Code here and press the Tab key.

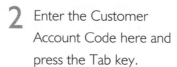

3 Click on the transaction you want to mark as disputed.

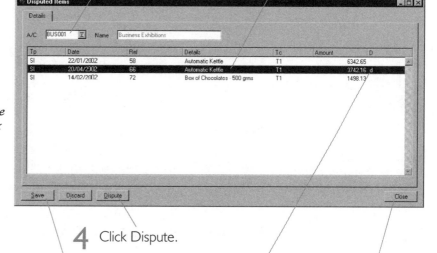

Use the Dispute button to mark or unmark an invoice as disputed.

4 Click Dispute.

5 Note that the transaction is now marked as 'd'.

Remember that if you're using Standard VAT, any invoices that you mark as disputed will still be included in the VAT Return.

6 Click Save to record the transaction.

7 Click Close to return to the Customers window, then Close again.

Customer Reports and Phone

The arrows on the Customers toolbar let you scroll across all available buttons.

Also use this report window to create, edit or delete Customer Reports.

An additional Criteria box may appear for some reports for you to enter ranges, such as Customer Reference etc.

If your computer modem & telephone share the same line you can ring a customer using the Phone button from the Customers toolbar, then pick up your phone to talk to them.

To check if your modem is working correctly, do Steps 1 & 2 to open the Modem Properties box, then select the Diagnostics tab, click on the modem Com port, then click on More Info. If it is working an Info box appears, otherwise Windows displays an error message.

Sage Line 50 provides you with a wide range of ready-designed customer reports to suit the majority of needs. To print or view a customer report, do the following:

1 Click on the Reports button in the Customers window.

2 Select the report you require from the Customer Reports list.

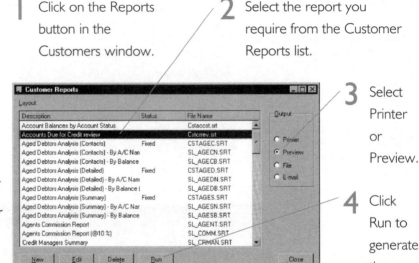

3 Select Printer or Preview.

4 Click Run to generate the report.

5 After printing Close each window.

Phone

With Sage Line 50 version 8, you do not need to set up the Com port before you can use the Phone facility. Line 50 detects the Com Port set up on your computer by interfacing directly with your operating system.

If you do not have modem facilities installed, Line 50 displays an error message. By default, the F11 key is set up by Line 50 to open the Control Panel so that you can check if your computer has a modem installed, as follows:

1 Press the F11 key to bring up the Windows Control Panel.

2 Double-click on the Modems icon to open the Modem Properties box.

Modems

3 The General tab displays if a modem is fitted in your computer.

Customer Letters and Labels

Remember to select a customer from the list before clicking the Letters button.

To send the same letter (e.g., change of address) to all your customers, first deselect all customers using the Clear button in the Customers window before carrying out Steps 2–7.

To avoid wasting paper, always use the Output, Preview option to check all letters and reports prior to printing.

To help speed up the process of sending correspondence to customers, use the standard layout label files to print out their names and addresses on predefined labels, or alternatively, create your own.

To produce labels for all your customers in one go clear any selected customers before pressing the Labels button on the Customers toolbar.

Occasionally you may have a need to send standard information to a customer, such as change of address, or to chase up an overdue payment. All of the necessary information needed for these letters is taken from your records.

A number of the more common standard letters are provided with Sage Line 50, but alternatively there is also the option to create new ones. The new letters can be stored for future use.

1 From the Customers window, select the customer or customers you want to send a letter to.

2 Click the Letters button on the Customers toolbar to bring up the Customer Letters list.

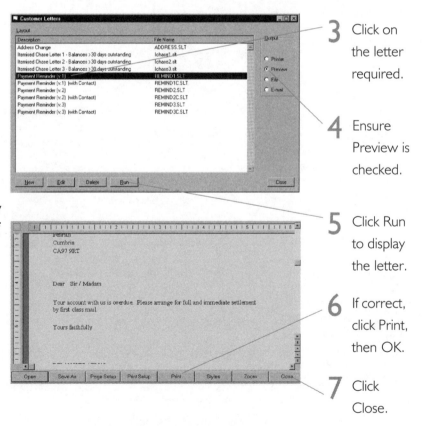

3 Click on the letter required.

4 Ensure Preview is checked.

5 Click Run to display the letter.

6 If correct, click Print, then OK.

7 Click Close.

The Customer Statement

To keep customers up to date about their financial position, customer statements should be sent out on a regular basis, normally once a month. The statement shows details of all recorded customer transactions, together with a balance figure.

You can also use the Customer Statement window to delete statements no longer required, or to modify and design your own statements.

1 From the Customers window click on the Statements button to bring up the Customer Statements window.

If you need a copy of the statement saving on disk use the Save As button in the statement preview window and give the statement a file name. You can then open and print the statement at a later date, if required.

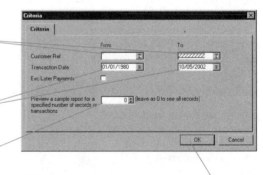

2 Choose the statement layout you require.

3 Ensure Preview is checked.

4 Click Run to bring up the Criteria box.

Sage Line 50 remembers which layout you used the last time you printed customer statements.

5 Enter Customer Reference range.

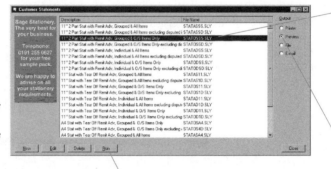

6 Enter Transaction Date From & To.

7 Click OK to preview statement.

To preview a sample report, simply enter number of records required in the box provided.

8 Use the Zoom button on the preview to zoom in or out if you need to check any statement details.

9 When satisfied, click Print to print the statement, then Close all windows.

The Supplier Ledger

This chapter shows you how to create and maintain supplier records within the Suppliers (Purchase) Ledger. Through recording invoices and credit notes you receive you can see how much you owe, when these payments are due and any disputed items. You will learn how to view details of any invoices received and payments made to suppliers using tables, graphs and reports.

Covers

Chapter Three

The Supplier Toolbar

The Supplier toolbar has many similar buttons to the Customer toolbar, and again provides you with facilities for setting up records, checking supplier activity, recording invoices, credit notes and reporting.

 Creates a new Supplier Record.

 Opens a Supplier Record.

 View Supplier Activity.

 View Supplier Aged Balances.

 Record Supplier Invoices.

 Record Supplier Credit Notes.

 Opens the Disputed Items window.

 To Automatically Dial a Supplier.

 To Print Supplier Labels.

 To Print Standard Letters to Suppliers.

 To Run Supplier Reports.

Creating Supplier Records

Until you are familiar with Sage Line 50, use the New wizard for simple step by step instructions for entering a new supplier record.

Within this window you can view, edit or delete a supplier record. A new supplier record can also be added if you have all of the details to hand. To add a new supplier first select Suppliers from the Sage Line 50 toolbar, then do the following:

1 Click on Record to bring up the Supplier Record window.

Always start with the A/C when entering a new record.

2 Use Details to enter supplier information, such as name, address and contact details.

3 Use the O/B button to enter an Opening Balance where required.

To help save time later, enter accurately as much detail into the record as possible.

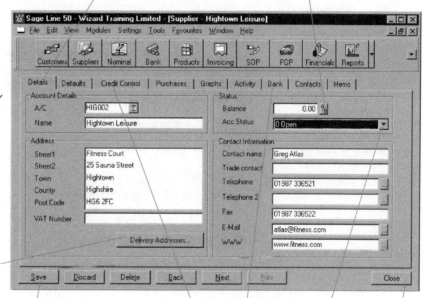

Sage Line 50 version 7 & 8 allow you to record multiple delivery addresses and associated contact details for your suppliers. Click on the Delivery Addresses button to bring up the display window, from where you can Add, Edit or Delete addresses.

4 Use the Credit Control tab to enter any agreed credit terms.

5 Select Account Status from this drop down box.

6 Enter supplier Bank details for payment transfers.

7 Click Save to store the Customer Record.

8 Enter a new record or click Close to finish.

Using Search

This useful Search feature is also available within other program windows, such as Customers, Products, Nominal and Invoicing etc.

The Search function available within the suppliers window can help save you valuable time when searching for specific information regarding supplier transactions. The following example shows you how to produce a list of suppliers you owe money to:

1 Click the Search button in the bottom left hand corner of the Suppliers window to bring up the Search window.

You can also use Search from the Customers window as a quick means of looking something up about your customers, such as a list of those who have exceeded their credit limit, or whose accounts are on hold. You can even use Search to search for a supplier or customer if, say, you only have a single item of detail to hand, such as a telephone number or department, provided this information has been entered when setting up the record.

2 Click here and select Where.

3 Select Balance in this field.

4 Select Greater than here.

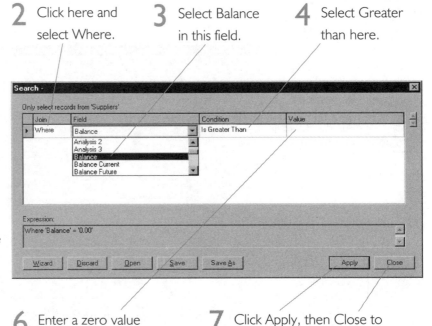

6 Enter a zero value in this field

7 Click Apply, then Close to return to the Suppliers window.

To search using part information, select the Is Equal To condition and preceed the Value with the symbol $. For example, use $W1 and the field Account Address Line 5 to search for all Suppliers in the London W1 area.

8 Note that only records matching the search are displayed. The title bar indicates Search is applied.

9 To cancel the search and show all records, click the icon here.

Supplier Activity

To view this screen from the Supplier Record window, enter the A/C for the supplier required (if none selected) and then click on the Activity tab.

You can also view activity by double-clicking on a record and selecting the Activity tab.

Use the Tidy List button to clear all transaction sub-items from view.

Note that the following codes identify the transaction type:

PI = Purchase Invoice.

PP = Purchase Payment.

PC = Purchase Credit Note.

PD = Discount on a Purchase Payment.

PA = Purchase Payment on Account.

Further supplier activity information is available through the supplier reports.

This feature enables you to view each supplier's transactions in detail. If less complete information is required, you can define a transaction or date range to limit the view:

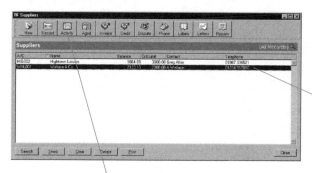

1 From the Suppliers window, click on the supplier you want to look at.

2 Click on Activity.

3 In the next box enter the transaction/date range and transaction type.

4 Click OK to bring up the Activity window.

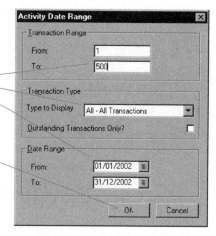

5 Double-click a transaction for more details.

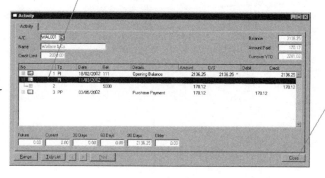

6 Click Close to return to the Suppliers window.

Supplier Aged Balance

The age period is set through Supplier Defaults from the Settings menu. You can base it on either calendar months or a period of days, specified by you. Remember also that ageing is relative to the program date.

Aged balance is the term given to the time lapse of outstanding debt, whether owed *to* or *by* you. Sage Line 50 lets you view the amount of money you owe your Suppliers, grouped on the age of the debt. It is common practice for businesses to give 30 days credit, but other terms are sometimes negotiated. Sage Line 50 default aged periods are 30, 60 and 90 days.

1 From the Suppliers window, click on the supplier you require and select the Aged button from the toolbar.

2 Enter appropriate dates here.

If you need to enter a date only a few days either side of that displayed simply use the cursor up or down keys on the keyboard.

3 Click OK to display the Aged Balances Report.

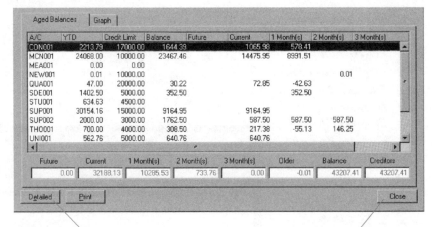

From November 1998 legislation took effect that enables small businesses (less than 50 employees) to charge interest on late payments from large businesses.

4 To see the transactions which make up the aged balance click Detailed.

5 Close each window when finished.

Recording Supplier Invoices

Invoices received from your suppliers can be entered a few at a time using the Batch Supplier Invoices window. You have full flexibility using this option, such as posting each invoice item to a different nominal account if need be, or allocating to a different VAT code, such as from default VAT to zero VAT. To enter invoices, do the following:

1 From the Suppliers window click Invoice to bring up the Batch Supplier Invoices window.

2 Type the supplier's account code here or use the Finder button.

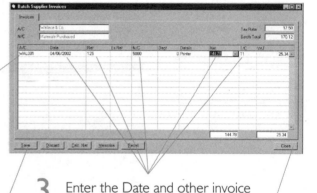

Remember that with batch invoices, no printouts are generated of the transaction entered. Use activity reports if you require hardcopy.

3 Enter the Date and other invoice details, then check the Nominal (N/C) and Tax (T/C) codes and amend if necessary.

As with a customer, if you are in dispute with a supplier over an invoice, you can mark it as disputed. See page 29.

4 When all details are correct and all invoices have been entered, click Save to post the details.

5 Click Close to return to the Suppliers window.

'Posting' means updating the Nominal ledger and relevant supplier's details. If you do not wish to save this batch, choose the Discard button to clear the data and start again.

6 Note that the Supplier's record now displays the new balance, then click Close again.

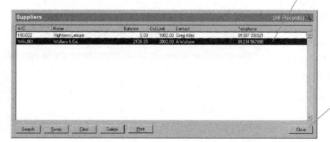

Recording Supplier Credit Notes

Occasionally goods ordered from suppliers may arrive damaged or incomplete. The supplier issues you a credit note reducing the amount owed. Credit notes are recorded using the Credit option from the Suppliers window.

If a credit note contains a number of items, for your benefit it is advisable to enter each transaction individually, but giving them the same account code, date and reference. Sage Line 50 will group these together and list them as a single credit note. You can then view the note in detail using Activity from the Suppliers window.

To see if there is more detail to an entry, just double-click on that entry line.

It is always advisable to check the changes you have made by noting the before and after outstanding balance. This will save time later should a mistake have been made.

The audit trail transaction code for a purchase credit note is PC.

It is useful to enter the invoice number that the credit note refers to in the Reference (Refn) box for identification. This will appear in the details under Financials.

I To record a credit note, from the Suppliers window click Credit.

2 Enter the supplier Account Code. Use the Finder button if you don't have the code.

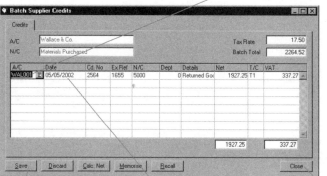

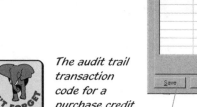

3 Enter the credit note date.

4 Enter the remaining details and check that they are correct.

5 Click Save to update the nominal ledger and record the credit details.

6 Click Close to return to the Suppliers window.

7 Note that the outstanding balance has changed and click Close.

Supplier Letters and Labels

As with Customers, Sage Line 50 includes the facility to produce preformatted letters and labels for your suppliers. You can create whatever standard letters or label layouts you wish. All necessary address information etc. is taken from the stored supplier details.

To produce the standard letter informing suppliers of your change of address, do the following:

To produce letters or labels for certain suppliers only, click on those suppliers to select them in the Suppliers window before carrying out Steps 1–5. If, however, you want to print letters or labels for all your suppliers, ensure none are selected by clicking on the Clear button in the Suppliers window.

1 From the Suppliers window click Letters to bring up the Supplier Letters window.

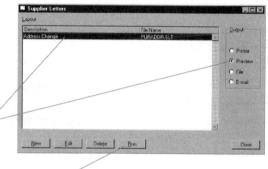

2 Click on the letter required and ensure Preview is checked.

3 Click Run.

4 Check the letters and click Print, then OK in the Printer box.

The credit control tab window has an option to Restrict mailing. Use this to control who you send mailshots to.

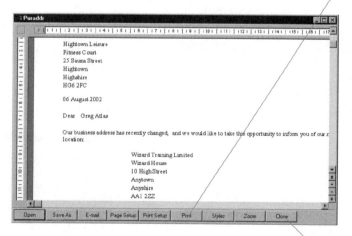

Always remember to check that the correct paper, labels and printer type have been selected before printing if you want to avoid wasting time and paper.

5 When finished, Close all windows.

Labels

To produce address labels for your suppliers, select the Labels button from the Suppliers window then carry out Steps 2–5 as above.

Supplier Reports

Use the arrow button on the Suppliers toolbar to scroll across to the Reports button.

You can generate a wide range of detailed reports about your suppliers. These reports are produced from the information you entered about suppliers and their transactions. Whilst Sage Line 50 already has a considerable number of reports set up, if any further reports are required you can create them using the Report Designer (see Chapter Twelve). To run or view a supplier report:

A Criteria box will appear when you click Run on most reports for you to enter ranges, such as Supplier Reference, Transaction Date etc.

1 Click on the Reports button in the Suppliers window.

2 Select the report you require from the Supplier Reports list.

3 Select Printer or Preview.

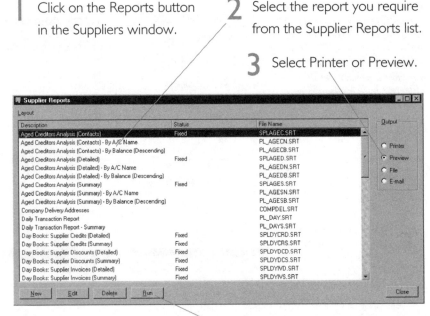

From the Supplier Reports window you can also edit or delete an existing report or create a new one.

4 Click Run to generate the report.

5 If a Criteria box appears, enter the From and To details, then click OK.

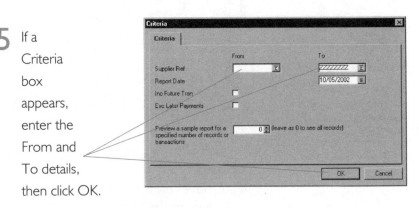

If you want to use the phone facility, you must select a Supplier before clicking the Phone button.

6 After printing, Close all windows.

The Nominal Ledger

This chapter explains the important role played by the Nominal Ledger and how its accounts detail the flow of money in and out of the business. You will be shown how to analyse these account transactions using tables, graphs and transaction activity reports so you can control and monitor finances through making informed business decisions. You can even tailor your own Nominal Ledger set of accounts to meet specific business needs.

Covers

Chapter Four

The Nominal Toolbar

The Nominal toolbar buttons provide you with facilities for setting up records, viewing account activity, making journal entries, setting up prepayments and accruals, working on the chart of accounts and reporting.

 Creates a new Nominal Account.

 Opens a Nominal Record.

 View a Nominal Account's Activity.

 Enter Journal double-entries.

 Process Nominal Ledger Reversals.

 Enter Nominal Ledger Prepayments.

 Enter Nominal Ledger Accrual.

 Opens the Chart of Accounts.

 To Run Nominal Ledger Reports.

The Nominal Ledger

To create a new nominal account, click the New button from the Nominal window.

The Nominal Ledger, also referred to as the General Ledger, is a grouped analysis of your sales and purchase transactions. For example, when a sales or purchase invoice is posted to the sales or purchase ledger, Sage Line 50 records it in the Nominal Ledger against the appropriate Nominal account number.

It therefore contains all the accounts for your business, e.g., sales, purchases, expenses, VAT, cash and bank, sundry income, fixed assets, liabilities, capital and owner's drawings, etc. However, it does not keep details of debtors and creditors. These are held in the respective sales and purchase ledgers.

Click on a record to select or to deselect it. Use the Clear button to deselect all selected records.

The Nominal accounts let you see quickly where your money is. Information from here is used in the production of management reports to tell you how your business is performing.

Standard nominal accounts for Sage Line 50 are:

- *Asset Accounts from 0001 to 1999*
- *Liability Accounts from 2000 to 3999*
- *Income Accounts from 4000 to 4999*
- *Purchase Accounts from 5000 to 5999*
- *Direct Expenses from 6000 to 6999*
- *Overheads from 7000 to 9999*

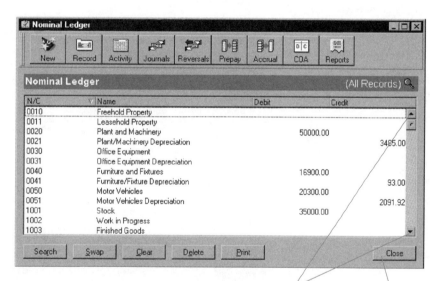

1 Click Nominal from the Sage Line 50 toolbar to view the Nominal Ledger.

2 Use scroll bar to view range of accounts.

3 Click Close when finished.

Search on Name to quickly locate a particular Nominal Code.

In Sage Line 50, a standard set of nominal accounts are created upon installation, unless in the Startup Wizard you decided to create your own nominal structure. Note that the latter option only creates the Control Accounts for you.

Nominal Records

Check your business performance by initially entering monthly budget and prior year values, then regularly comparing these against the actual value.

You can tailor the nominal accounts to exactly meet your needs by using the Nominal Record window. You have the facility to add, edit and delete nominal accounts as well as viewing transactions posted to each account on a monthly basis.

Using the Record window you can also set budget values for each month of your financial year for a particular nominal account. You can also compare the actual monthly figures against the budget values to keep track of how close you are to meeting targets. To add a nominal account record, do the following:

You can edit a Nominal Account to suit your needs. Simply use the Finder button for Step 2 to locate the N/C, then type any changes in the Name box and click on the Save button.

1 Click Record from the Nominal Ledger to bring up the Nominal Record window.

2 In the Details tab box, enter the new nominal account code here.

You cannot delete a Nominal Code whilst there is still a balance on it.

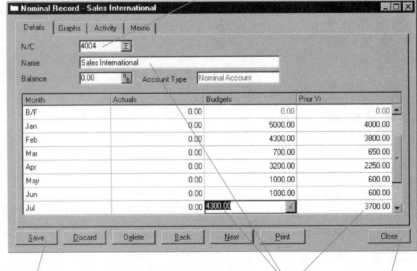

The New account details must first be saved before an Opening Balance can be entered.

3 Press the Tab key and note that this is a New Account.

4 Enter new account Name, Budget and Prior Year values.

5 Click Save to store details or Discard to start again.

6 Click Close to return to the Nominal Ledger.

Viewing Nominal Transactions

You can view your Nominal Ledger transactions by using:

- Graphs.

- Activity reports.

- Table formats.

Transaction Analysis using Graphs

A range of 2D and 3D charts is available in Sage Line 50 to visually compare your current year's trading against the previous year and any budgets you have put in place.

You can save the graph to disk as a chart file. Click on Disk icon and enter a file name.

Use this button to switch between 2D and 3D graph.

You can change what you view on the graph by clicking on the Options button and altering the View or Compare selection.

You can include Sage Line 50 graphs in other documents you may wish to produce. Simply use the Camera button to copy the graph, open your application and use the paste function to insert it into your other document.

1 From the Nominal Ledger window, select the nominal account you wish to view.

2 Click Record, then select the Graphs tab to display data in graphical form.

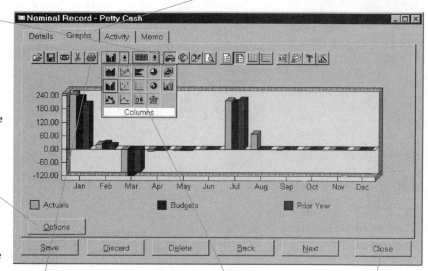

3 To choose a different type of graph, click here, then click on the graph required.

4 Click on the Printer button to print out the graph.

5 Click Close to return to the Nominal Ledger window.

Viewing Nominal Account Activity

You will occasionally need to view transactions that have been posted to the nominal ledger accounts. To do this from the Nominal Ledger window:

Transactions already cleared from the audit trail are shown as a single carried forward total and displayed as an Opening Balance (O/BAL).

1 Click on the nominal account you wish to view.

2 Click on the Activity button to bring up the Activity Date Range box.

3 Enter the appropriate Transaction/Date ranges and Type to Display.

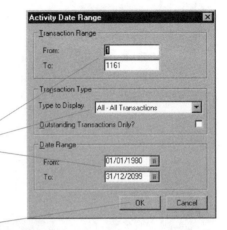

Each line of the Activity list box represents a single invoice, credit note, payment on account or receipt.

4 Click OK to display Activity.

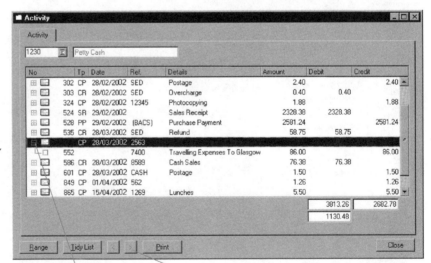

You can select more than one account to view at a time and simply use the '<' and '>' arrow buttons to scroll through them.

For a printout of the Nominal Activity refer to the Reports section.

5 Double-click a transaction to view any further details.

6 Use the arrow buttons to view other nominal accounts, if more than one is selected in Step 1.

7 Click Close to return to the Nominal Ledger.

Transaction Codes

Transactions in the Activity window are identified by a type (Tp) or transaction code, allocated by Sage Line 50. The following is a list of transaction codes used:

The Ref. column in the Activity window shows the reference given to the transaction when it was posted.

BR (Bank Receipt)	SD (Discount on Sales Receipt)
BP (Bank Payment)	SA (Sales Receipt on Account)
CP (Cash Payment)	PI (Purchase Invoice)
CR (Cash Receipt)	PP (Purchase Payment)
JD (Journal Debit)	PC (Purchase Credit)
JC (Journal Credit)	PD (Discount on Purchase Payment)
SI (Sales Invoice)	PA (Purchase Payment on Account)
SR (Sales Receipt)	VP (Visa Credit Payments)
SC (Sales Credit)	VR (Visa Credit Receipts)

You can tell at a glance if Search is being applied to a list because it will not display the words All Records on the right side of the title bar.

Using Search

It is sometimes handy to reduce the number of records displayed in the Nominal Ledger window or on your reports to only those that match a specific criteria. This will save you having to look through too many records just to find the information you need. For example, this is how to list only control accounts in the Nominal Ledger window:

The Number (No.) column shows the transaction number in the Audit Trail. You will need this number if you wish to amend or delete a transaction using the File, Maintenance, Corrections option.

1 Click Search in the Nominal Ledger window.

2 Select Where here.

3 Choose Account Type Code here.

4 Select Equal To.

Search remains applied to a list until you click the Search icon on the right hand side of the title bar:

5 Select Control Account from the list.

6 Click Apply to action.

7 Click Close.

The Journal

The rules for debits and credits are: Debit the account which receives the value; Credit the account which gives the value.

The Journal allows you to make transfers between any of your nominal account codes regardless of type (Asset, Liability, Income or Expenditure), provided you adhere to double-entry bookkeeping principles. It lets you enter transactions which may not be covered within the standard Sage Line 50 facilities.

It is a useful source of reference for these non-regular transactions and can reduce errors by providing a list (audit trail) for checking purposes. Examples of these transactions include correction of errors and transfer of monies, as well as the purchase and sale of fixed assets on credit.

If you use the journal to record transfer of monthly salary payments, use the Monthly Salary skeleton journal provided by Sage Line 50.

As stated, the Journal follows double-entry bookkeeping principles i.e., the value of the credit transaction must equal the value of the debit transaction. Each line of the Journal Entry table represents a single transaction; therefore there must be at least two transactions in the journal (a credit and a debit).

For details about the skeleton journals set up for you in Sage Line 50, see the Library Help and Search for Skeleton.

However, this does not mean that you must post a single credit item for every single debit item. You can, for example, post several debits but only one balancing credit, and vice versa. Provided the net difference between your postings is always zero (i.e. the total value of credits equals the total value of debits), you can then post the Journal.

'Skeleton' Journals

For journals that you make regularly, payments from a bank to a credit card account for example, Sage Line 50 lets you save the details of that journal entry so that you can use it the next time without having to enter it all again. This is called a 'skeleton'. Some skeleton journals were set up at installation, such as the VAT Liability Transfer Journal.

If you post a journal entry incorrectly, from Line 50 v8 you can use the Reversals button from the Journals toolbar to remove the entry. You can then simply re-enter the journal correctly. Just click on the Reversals button and follow the prompts to print the Nominal Ledger Day Book and backup your data before you process the reversal.

To save a skeleton journal, click on the Memorise button after you have set up the journal. To load a skeleton journal, click on the Recall button, select the journal you need and click on the Load button. You can even load one of the skeleton journals provided by Line 50, modify it to suit your needs, then save it.

Reversals

In Line 50 v8 you can reverse an incorrectly posted journal entry. Use Sage Help for a full explanation of reversing a journal.

Reversals

Making a Journal Entry

For a journal entry, VAT is neither calculated for you nor posted to the VAT control account.

Here is an example of how you would make a journal entry for a transfer of funds between your bank account and business building society account.

1 From the Nominal Ledger toolbar, click Journal.

2 Use the Calendar button if a different date is required.

If you use a journal entry regularly save it as a Skeleton using the Memorise button, so you can re-create it quickly and easily later.

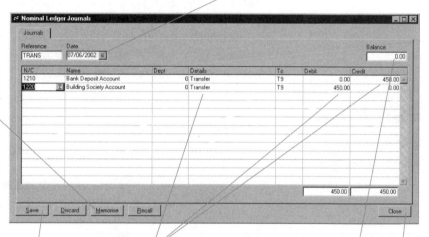

Each line of the Journal display represents a single transaction. There must be at least two transactions in the journal, a debit and a credit.

3 Enter details for both the credit and debit transactions. Reference is optional.

4 Note, the default Tax code of T9 is entered for you by Sage Line 50.

5 Check total Debit and Credit are equal and a zero balance is displayed in the Balance box.

Before saving the Journal, always ensure the Balance box shows zero. If the value of the credit transactions does not equal the value of the debit transactions, then Sage Line 50 issues a warning and will not let you save the Journal.

6 Click Save to process your journal or Discard to cancel.

7 Click Close to return to Nominal Ledger window.

Note that Sage Line 50 will not automatically calculate VAT, or post it to the VAT Control Account. If VAT is required, enter each VAT element as a separate line, with a debit or credit to the appropriate VAT Control Account.

Setting up Prepayments

Just click on the Wizard Button in the Prepayments window to let the Prepayments Wizard guide you through setting up a prepayment.

To adjust statements and reports for any payments which have to be made in advance, for example rent or insurance, there is a Prepayments option available from the Nominal Ledger window. This allows for a payment to be shown as spread over the number of months it refers to, not just the month it was paid in.

After setting up a prepayment, when you run the Month End procedure the correct monthly figure is posted to the appropriate account. All you have to do is to remember to post a suitable payment for the full amount (i.e. from the bank) to the appropriate nominal account.

Use Key F6 to save time and reduce errors when copying data from a previous transaction row.

2 Enter relevant nominal account code or use the Finder button.

1 From the Nominal Ledger toolbar, click Prepay to bring up the Prepayments window.

You will need to post a payment to the Prepayments account for the full amount.

3 Enter a suitable description.

4 Enter total net value of prepayment.

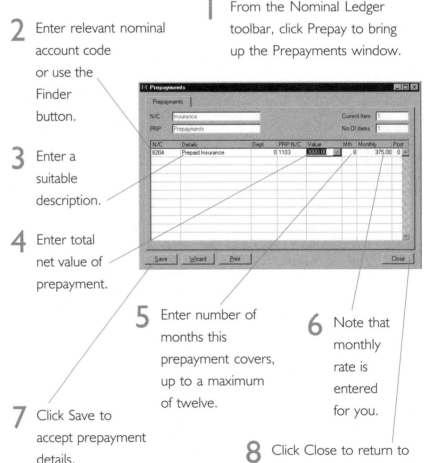

No accounting takes place when prepayment details are saved. Journal Entry postings are only made when the Month End, Post Prepayments option is run.

5 Enter number of months this prepayment covers, up to a maximum of twelve.

6 Note that monthly rate is entered for you.

7 Click Save to accept prepayment details.

8 Click Close to return to Nominal Ledger window.

Setting up Accruals

The Post column shows how many postings have been made using the Month End Post prepayment option.

The Accruals option allows the accounts to be adjusted for any payments you make in one accounting period which in fact relate to a previous period, such as a gas or electricity bill.

In this example, the transaction would be entered using the Accrual and Gas or Electricity accounts when the charges actually fall due, but when the bill is paid, the payment transaction is applied to the Accrual account and not the Gas or Electricity account.

As with the prepayments option, the accruals are posted as part of your month end procedure using the Period End, Month End option. This procedure automatically updates the audit trail and nominal accounts records.

You will need to post a payment to the Accruals account for the full amount.

2 Enter relevant nominal account code, or use the Finder button.

I From the Nominal Ledger window click Accrual.

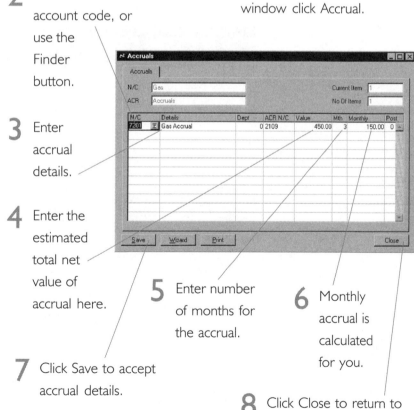

No accounting takes place when accrual details are saved. Journal Entry postings are only made when the Month End, Post Accruals option is run.

3 Enter accrual details.

4 Enter the estimated total net value of accrual here.

5 Enter number of months for the accrual.

6 Monthly accrual is calculated for you.

If you have already set up some Accrual entries, these appear in the Accruals window when it opens. Just add your new Accrual at the end of the list.

7 Click Save to accept accrual details.

8 Click Close to return to Nominal Ledger window.

The Chart of Accounts

The chart of Accounts is subdivided into the following default report category types:

Profit & Loss
- *Sales*
- *Purchases*
- *Direct Expenses*
- *Overheads.*

Balance Sheet
- *Fixed Assets*
- *Current Assets*
- *Current Liabilities*
- *Long Term Liabilities*
- *Capital & Reserves.*

During installation, Sage Line 50 created a simple Chart of Accounts suitable for standard reporting, such as Profit and Loss, Balance Sheet, Budget and Prior Year Reports.

It may be that the default account names are not suitable for your business, so the Chart of Accounts can be customised to meet your business requirements. New category types can be introduced into the accounts or current categories edited to reflect, for example, the actual items sold within your business.

1 To examine the Chart of Accounts' facilities, click COA from the Nominal Ledger window.

2 If you want to look at a chart, select it from the list and click Edit.

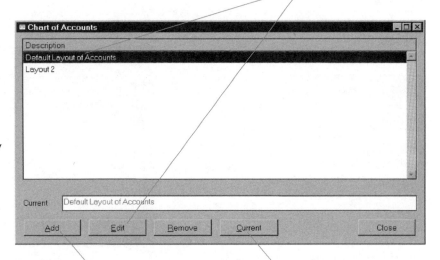

Every time you run your financial reports, you can select another layout if you wish.

Check that the name of the layout you selected appears automatically in the 'Current' text box.

3 To create a new Chart of Accounts, click the Add button.

5 When finished, click Close to return to the Nominal Ledger window.

4 To use a particular Chart of Accounts simply highlight it from the list and click the Current button.

If you elected to create your own chart of accounts during the Startup Wizard, the default chart of accounts will not contain any category accounts.

Creating a Chart of Accounts Layout

If you need to add a new Chart of Accounts layout, do the following:

1 Click COA from the Nominal Ledger window.

2 Click Add in the Chart of Accounts window.

3 Enter name of your new Chart of Accounts layout.

4 Click Add to continue.

When you run your financial reports, the value of each nominal account within each category account will be added together.

5 Click on a category and change its description to that required in your financial reports.

6 Enter (or amend) the headings for each range of nominal accounts in the selected category.

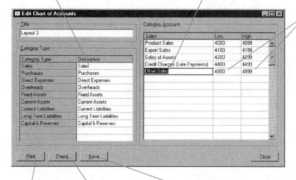

7 Set range of nominal accounts to be included for each selected category in Low & High boxes.

When entering nominal account ranges in Low/High boxes, type the same number in both boxes if only one code exists.

8 Click Check to see if you've made any errors.

9 Click Save, or Close to discard.

Use the Check button to find any nominal account errors in your new layout.

10 To print your Chart of Accounts, click Print, then Run.

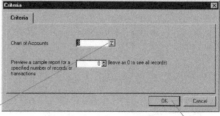

11 Select required chart in the Criteria box.

12 Click OK to print.

Nominal Reports

To print or preview reports using the nominal data already entered into the system, use the Reports option from the Nominal Ledger. Sage Line 50 already supplies a considerable number of pre-installed reports to suit most needs, but you can create additional custom reports using the Report Designer. See Chapter 12 for more details on creating reports.

Also use the Nominal Reports window to delete a report or if you need to create or edit reports.

To print a Nominal Ledger report, do the following:

1 From the Nominal Ledger toolbar, click Reports.

Use the Criteria button on the Nominal Ledger window to make report generation easier by restricting the selection of nominal account codes to specified criteria.

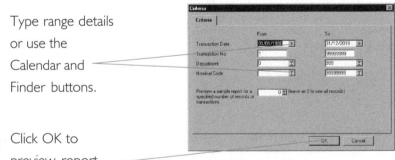

2 Click on report layout required.

3 Check Output is set to Preview.

4 Click Run to bring up the Criteria box.

You may sometimes find it easier to select nominal accounts from the Nominal Ledger window instead of entering them in the Criteria box.

5 Type range details or use the Calendar and Finder buttons.

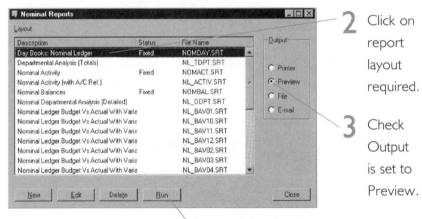

6 Click OK to preview report.

7 If a printout is required, click on the Print button.

8 Click Close to return to the Layout window.

9 Close all windows to finish.

The Bank

This chapter shows you how to maintain your bank account records and transactions. This includes deposits, payments, transfer of money between bank accounts and adjustments to show bank charges and interest received. It also covers reconciling your statements, processing recurring entries and the automatic production of cheques.

Covers

Chapter Five

The Bank Toolbar

This toolbar provides features for the recording and maintenance of bank transactions and records. You can perform adjustments, record the transfer of monies, enter receipts, produce statements and reports and even print cheques.

 Creates a new Bank Account.

 Opens a Bank Record.

 Opens Bank Account Reconciliation.

 Record Bank Payments.

 Record Supplier Payments.

 To Print Bank Remittances.

 To Record a Batch Purchase Payment.

 Record Money Received.

 Record Customer Receipts.

 Make Bank Transfers.

 Opens Recurring Entries Window.

 To Print Bank Statements.

 To Print Cheques.

 To Run Bank Account Reports.

Bank Accounts

To guide you through creating a new Bank account, use the New Wizard from the Bank Toolbar.

There are three types of Bank accounts used in Sage Line 50: the Bank Account, Cash Account and Credit Card Account.

The Bank account option treats both Bank and Building Societies as bank accounts. Three bank accounts have been automatically set up to include a bank current account, a bank deposit account and a building society account.

A single Cash Account called Petty Cash has been set up, but other cash accounts can be added, for example, Emergency Cash or Additional Travel Expenses etc.

The arrows on the Customers toolbar let you scroll across all available buttons.

The facility to record your credit card bank details is available and allows you to monitor any credit card transactions you have made and keep track of your money. Two credit card accounts have already been set up for use.

To view the Bank account window:

From the Sage Line 50 Toolbar click on the Bank icon.

Have your current bank balance to hand when creating new Bank records.

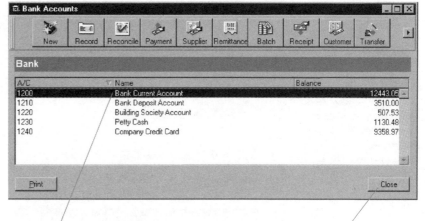

Sage Line 50 treats both Bank and Building Societies as Bank accounts.

2 Click once on the bank account required, then click on the appropriate icon for the function you wish to carry out.

3 When finished, click Close.

Bank, Cash and Credit Accounts

Sage Line 50 provides three types of bank accounts:

Use the Bank Record Wizard to guide you through setting up a new bank account.

- Bank Account (includes both bank deposit and current account, plus a building society account).

Refer to Chapter Thirteen for more information on entering opening balances.

- Cash Account (named Petty Cash).

- Credit Card Account (company credit card and credit card receipts).

These accounts can be edited to match your own details. Accounts can also be added or deleted. To set up your Bank account details:

Your bank accounts and financial reports use nominal codes 1200 to 1299.

1 From the Bank Accounts window, select account type required and click on the Record icon.

2 Make changes if necessary here.

3 Click here to enter Current Balance. The Opening Balance Setup box appears.

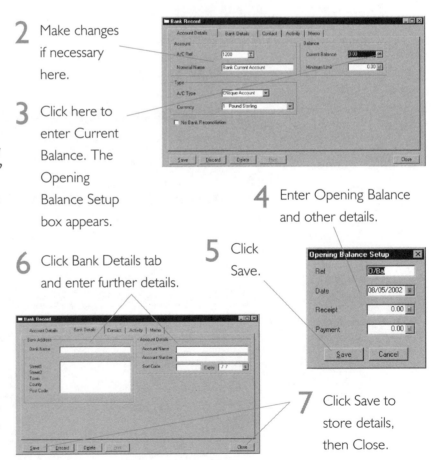

In the Opening Balances Setup window, if you have money in your bank account enter it in the Receipt box, if you are overdrawn in your bank account enter the value in the Payment box.

4 Enter Opening Balance and other details.

5 Click Save.

6 Click Bank Details tab and enter further details.

Should the minimum balance fall below the figure entered, it will be displayed in red in the Bank Accounts window.

7 Click Save to store details, then Close.

Recording Bank Payments

Any payments to your suppliers should be entered using the Supplier option as this will automatically bring up any outstanding invoices when the supplier's account reference is entered.

For recording any non-invoiced or one-off payments use the Payment option from the Bank Accounts window. Sage Line 50 then makes it very easy for you to keep track of where your money goes – simply select the appropriate account, enter the payment and post it.

To record Bank payments:

1 Click Payment from the Bank Accounts window.

2 Use Finder button to enter Bank account code.

3 Enter Date and transaction Reference (if required).

If you only know the Gross value of the payment, simply enter it in the Net box and click on the Calc. Net button.

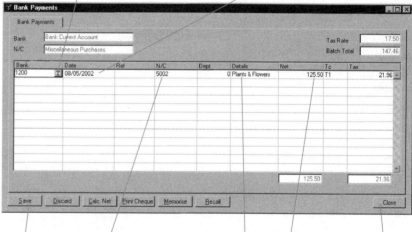

4 Enter a Nominal Code for the payment to be posted to, or use the Finder button.

5 Enter Details.

6 Enter amount (change Tax Code from default of T1 if necessary).

Use the Discard button if you want to clear the data and start again. Any entries already saved will not be cancelled.

7 Click Save to post details (update the nominal ledger and the Bank account).

8 Click Close to finish.

Supplier Invoice Payments

BEWARE *A warning appears if you try to pay a disputed invoice. Only when the invoice is paid in full does the disputed flag disappear.*

The Supplier option from the Bank Accounts toolbar will provide you with a detailed transaction list of any outstanding invoice items, credit notes and payments made on account to suppliers. To record payment of a supplier invoice do the following:

1 In the Bank Accounts window, select the account required (e.g., Bank Current Account) and click the Supplier button.

DON'T FORGET *Leave the cheque number blank if you intend using the Cheques option. Cheques will be automatically generated for you.*

2 Enter supplier account code.

3 Use Calendar button if payment date is different.

HOT TIP *Enter a discount value in the discount box, not a percentage, for any invoiced item. The Analysis Total box decreases by the discount value entered.*

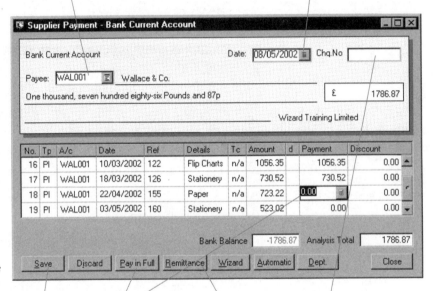

Supplier Payment - Bank Current Account

Bank Current Account   Date: 08/05/2002   Chq.No

Payee: WAL001   Wallace & Co.

One thousand, seven hundred eighty-six Pounds and 87p   £   1786.87

Wizard Training Limited

No.	Tp	A/c	Date	Ref	Details	Tc	Amount	d	Payment	Discount
16	PI	WAL001	10/03/2002	122	Flip Charts	n/a	1056.35		1056.35	0.00
17	PI	WAL001	18/03/2002	126	Stationery	n/a	730.52		730.52	0.00
18	PI	WAL001	22/04/2002	155	Paper	n/a	723.22		0.00	0.00
19	PI	WAL001	03/05/2002	160	Stationery	n/a	523.02		0.00	0.00

Bank Balance   -1786.87   Analysis Total   1786.87

Save   Discard   Pay in Full   Remittance   Wizard   Automatic   Dept.   Close

DON'T FORGET *You don't have to enter a value on the cheque: Sage Line 50 does it for you.*

5 Enter value in Payment box for part-payment or click on Pay in Full button to enter full amount.

4 Enter cheque number if required. (See the first DON'T FORGET icon in the margin.)

6 Repeat Step 5 for any remaining transactions.

HOT TIP *New in Sage Line 50 v8, the Remittance button has moved. Use the Remittance button on the Bank toolbar to quickly print a batch of remittances:*

Remittance

7 Click Remittance button to print remittance, but see HOT TIP in margin.

8 Click Save to save payment details and Close.

Batch Purchase Payments

You can pay a transaction in full or part.

You can list all outstanding purchase invoices, purchase credit notes and purchase payments on account for all suppliers using the Batch option from the Bank Accounts window. The transactions are sorted firstly by supplier and then by transaction number.

Outstanding transactions can be paid in three ways:

- All transactions paid in full.

- Individual transactions paid in full.

- Individual transactions paid in part.

To record full or part payments:

All outstanding transactions can be paid in full in one go using the Pay All button, but there will only be one posting.

1 From Bank Accounts select the account and click Batch.

2 To pay ALL outstanding transactions click Pay All.

If any transactions are in dispute a warning message appears.

Batch Purchase Payments

Outstanding Transactions

| Bank | Bank Current Account | | | | | | Date | 08/05/2002 |
| A/C | Wallace & Co. | | | | | | | |

No.	Tp	A/c	Date	Ref	Details	Tc	Amount	d	Payment	Discount
1	PI	WAL001	03/05/2002	111	Opening B/a	n/a	2136.25		0.00	0.00
15	PC	WAL001	18/02/2002			n/a	587.50		0.00	0.00
16	PI	WAL001	22/02/2002	122	Flip Charts	n/a	1056.35		0.00	0.00
17	PI	WAL001	18/03/2002	126	Stationery	n/a	730.52		0.00	0.00
18	PI	WAL001	22/04/2002	155	Paper	n/a	723.22		0.00	0.00
19	PI	WAL001	03/05/2002	160	Stationery	n/a	523.02		0.00	0.00

| Bank Balance | 0.00 | | | | | | Total | 0.00 |

| Save | Discard | Pay in Full | Pay All | Dept. | | | | Close |

Regularly check the values in the Total and Bank Balance boxes.

3 To make INDIVIDUAL full payments, select a transaction and click on the Pay in Full button.

4 For a PART PAYMENT simply enter the amount in the Payment box.

5 When finished, Click Save or Discard to start again.

6 Click Close.

Bank Receipts

To record any non-invoiced or miscellaneous payments you receive, the Receipts option from the Bank Accounts window is used. These items are allocated a specific nominal code for analysis purposes so a check can be made on monies received.

To enter receipt of money:

1 From the Bank Account window Click on the Receipt icon.

2 In the Bank Receipts window, select the appropriate Bank account.

3 Ensure the required Date is entered here.

4 Enter a Reference here, such as a cheque number.

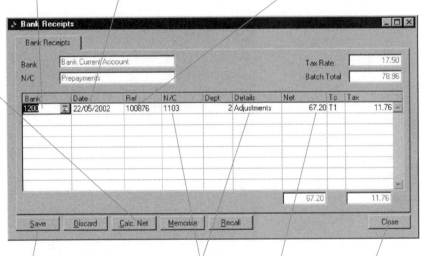

Bank	Date	Ref	N/C	Dept	Details	Net	Tc	Tax
1200	22/05/2002	100876	1103	2	Adjustments	67.20	T1	11.76

Bank: Bank Current Account   Tax Rate: 17.50
N/C: Prepayments   Batch Total: 78.96

67.20   11.76

5 Select a Nominal Account Code to post the receipt to and give details.

6 Enter Net value.

7 Repeat Steps 2–6 to record further receipts, then click Save to post transactions.

8 When finished, Close all windows.

Recording Customer Receipts

First enter the gross amount received in the Amount box, then check to ensure this equals the Analysis Total when you have finished.

The Customer option from the Bank Accounts window is used to record money received from your customers. When the customer's account reference is entered any outstanding invoices appear automatically in the Customer Receipt window.

To record full or part payments:

1 From the Bank Accounts window, select the bank account required and click Customer.

2 Enter a customer Account Code to display all items not fully paid for that customer.

3 Change Date if necessary and enter a paying in Reference if possible.

Use the Customers Receipt Wizard to help you record any cheques received for customer invoice payments, allocate credit notes and payments on account to invoices or to post a payment on account only.

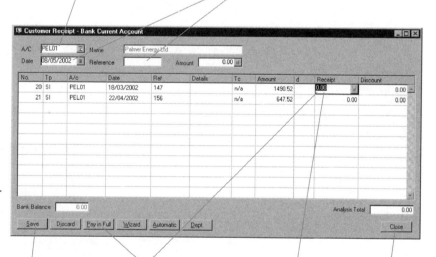

Customer Receipt - Bank Current Account

A/C: PEL01   Name: Palmer Energy Ltd
Date: 08/05/2002   Reference: Amount: 0.00

No.	Tp	A/c	Date	Ref	Details	T.c	Amount	d	Receipt	Discount
20	SI	PEL01	18/03/2002	147		n/a	1490.52		0.00	0.00
21	SI	PEL01	22/04/2002	156		n/a	647.52		0.00	0.00

Bank Balance: 0.00   Analysis Total: 0.00

[Save] [Discard] [Pay in Full] [Wizard] [Automatic] [Dept]   [Close]

You can pay an invoice in full or part but you cannot allocate an amount more than the item value.

Sage Line 50 automatically warns you of any disputed items.

4 If FULL payment has been received select a transaction and click Pay in Full.

5 If this is a PART payment enter the amount received here.

6 Enter any further receipts then click Save to process them or Discard to start again.

7 When finished, Close all windows.

Bank Transfers

There is also a Wizard to help you make a Bank Transfer.

Sometimes you will need to transfer money from one bank account to another. You can record this using the Transfer option from the Bank Accounts window or by making a journal entry.

To make a bank transfer do the following:

1 From the Bank Accounts window, select the bank you wish to move the money from.

You can also record a Bank Transfer through a journal entry.

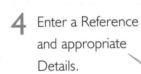

2 Click Transfer to bring up the Bank Transfer window.

The Reference details will be recorded in the audit Trail. You are allowed up to eight characters.

4 Enter a Reference and appropriate Details.

3 Enter Nominal Code of the Bank you are transferring to.

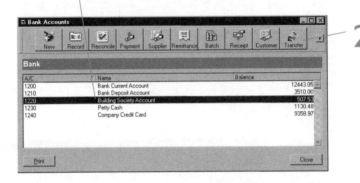

5 Check the correct date is entered in the Date box.

Sage Line 50 always enters today's date in the Date box, but this can be altered if necessary.

6 Enter transfer amount.

7 Click Save to process the transfer or Discard to start again.

8 Click Close to finish, then Close again.

Recurring Entries

Recurring entries need processing each month before you can run the Month or Year End procedures.

For payments which remain consistent and are paid on a monthly basis, for example rent and electricity, the Recurring option can be used from the Bank Accounts window. This feature is also useful for standing orders and direct debits and prevents payments such as these from being overlooked. Each month, these transactions need posting to update your banks and ledgers.

If there are any outstanding recurring entries, Sage Line 50 reminds you on startup and asks if you wish to post them. To add a recurring entry:

Sage Line 50 will only let you post journal credits when you post journal debits of the same value, and vice versa.

1 Select Recurring from the Bank Accounts window and Click Add.

2 Enter transaction type from the list box.

3 Enter the Bank Account Code.

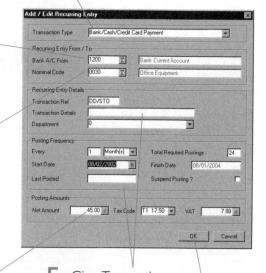

4 Enter a Nominal Code to post the transaction to.

The Last Posted box will remain blank until the new entry is saved and processed.

5 Give Transaction Reference/Details as required and enter Posting Frequency.

To stop a monthly payment, click the Suspend Posting box. This is handy for some payments which do not need posting every month.

6 Enter Net amount and check the Tax Code.

7 Click OK to return to the Recurring Entries window.

8 Click Process and Process All to process the recurring entries, then click Close to finish.

Generating Cheques

Use the Date Range check box to generate cheques between specified dates.

This is a relatively new feature within Sage Line 50 and offers the ability to print cheques automatically for a particular bank account. All Purchase Payments (type PP) and Purchase Payments on Account (type PA) transactions not previously printed and with blank references are listed in the Print Cheques window. This is how to print cheques using the cheque generator:

You can now print a cheque for a supplier without first having to set up an account.

1 From the Bank Accounts window, select the required bank account and click on the Cheques button.

2 Allocate a new Cheque Number if required.

If no transactions are selected, the program will print cheques for ALL the listed transactions.

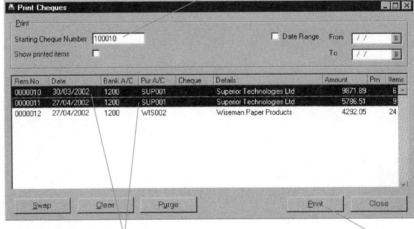

Sage Line 50 allocates to cheques unique, incrementing cheque numbers. When the cheques have been printed correctly, the next available cheque number is stored within the Bank record.

3 Select transactions requiring cheques.

4 Click Print.

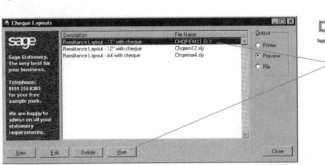

5 Select layout required, then click Run.

6 Click Yes if cheques printed correctly, then Close.

The Bank Statement

Sage Line 50 provides you with the facility to print your bank statements out at any time, showing all reconciled bank payments and receipts.

To use this facility effectively, you should make sure that you enter all Bank transactions accurately and completely so that the Sage Line 50 Bank statements match your actual bank statements.

These statements show the transactions made to and from each bank account, and prove useful for cross-referencing purposes when checking for any transaction omissions or additions. To print a report in bank statement format, do the following:

1 From the Bank Accounts window click on the Statement button to bring up the Criteria window.

2 Enter Transaction Date range.

3 Enter To and From Bank Ref's, using the Finder button for ease.

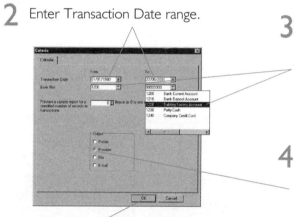

4 Select Preview from Output options.

You can also save the Bank Statement reports as a file for use at a later date. Simply click on the Save As button in the report preview window.

5 Click Run to preview statement.

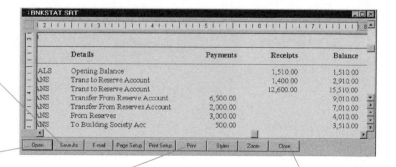

To bring up previously saved statements, Click Open and select the required statement from the list.

6 Click Print and OK from the print dialog box.

7 Click Close to return to the Bank Accounts window.

Bank Account Reconciliation

Before you select any transactions to reconcile, always check that the opening balance shown in the Bank Reconciliation window is the same as the opening balance on your actual bank statement.

Bank reconciliation is the process of matching up your computer bank records and transactions with those shown on your bank statements.

The Bank Reconciliation window displays transactions which have not been previously reconciled. After entering the date of the statement, you can work through your bank statement matching the transactions recorded in Sage Line 50. If necessary, you should make any adjustments needed to ensure that Sage Line 50 bank accounts accurately reflect the transactions processed by your actual bank. To reconcile a bank account:

1 From the Bank Accounts window select the bank account to be reconciled, then click Reconcile.

Press the F1 key or refer to Sage Help for additional information about bank reconciliation.

2 Enter the date of the actual bank statement and press Tab.

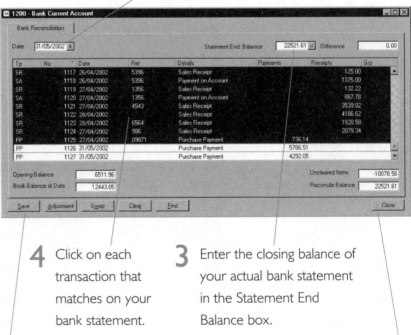

A bank account cannot be reconciled if the check box No Bank Reconciliation has been selected on the bank record.

To search for specific transactions, use the Find button.

4 Click on each transaction that matches on your bank statement.

3 Enter the closing balance of your actual bank statement in the Statement End Balance box.

5 If the Reconcile and Statement End balances match, click Save.

6 Click Close.

...cont'd

Thoroughly check all transactions on the bank statement against the Bank Reconciliation list. Check that the Reconcile Balance box matches the closing balance of your bank statement.

Bank reconciliation will only work correctly provided that a number of important rules are followed:

- The opening balance shown on the Bank Reconciliation window must match the opening balance on your actual bank statement.

If for some reason they are different, you will need to check why and make the necessary adjustments. One way of doing this is to view the selected bank's activity from within the nominal ledger. To see if a transaction has been reconciled or not, check the Bank column in the Audit Trail, where R = reconciled and N = not reconciled.

- Work through your actual bank statement progressively one line at a time, clicking on the corresponding transaction entry in the Bank reconciliation window to highlight it.

As you select each transaction you will see the Reconcile Balance change automatically.

- If you come across a transaction on your bank statement not shown in Sage Line 50, you should record this transaction immediately using the Adjustments facility.

- Check everything carefully. When you are satisfied that all necessary transactions for reconciliation have been selected and any adjustments made, the Difference box should show zero.

Making Adjustments

Use the Adjustments button or Bank Payments, Receipts and Transfers to record any additional transactions shown on your bank statement, e.g., bank charges, cashpoint withdrawals etc.

1 From the Reconciliation window, click on the Adjustment button.

2 Enter the Nominal Code of the account to receive the adjustment.

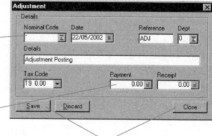

3 Enter adjustment details.

4 If correct click Save, then Close.

Bank Reports

When you have become familiar with the various reports you can save time by sending them straight to the printer without the need to preview. Select Printer instead of Preview in Step 3.

There is a wide range of ready-to-use bank reports provided by Sage Line 50. These reports outline your bank details and transactions and help you keep track of your bank finances. It is advisable that you regularly print out the standard reports, such as Day Books, once you have entered the relevant transactions.

1 From the Bank Accounts window, click Reports to bring up the Bank Reports window.

2 Click on the report required.

3 Ensure Preview is selected.

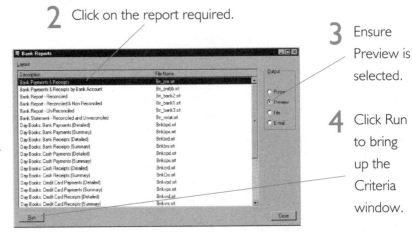

You can save a report as a file in a number of useful formats, such as Microsoft Write, Text file or Comma Separated Value (CSV).

4 Click Run to bring up the Criteria window.

5 Enter Criteria required for report.

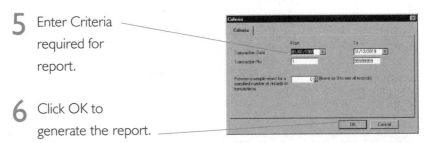

6 Click OK to generate the report.

If you chose to print the report, the Windows Print dialog box appears. Use this to select which pages to print and change your printer settings if necessary.

7 Click Print, then OK and Close.

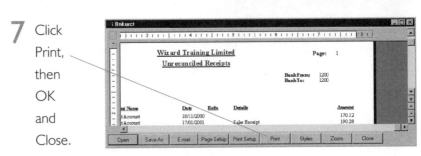

Products

This chapter shows you how to create and maintain records for products you buy and sell and how to set up product codes. These details, once recorded in the system, will be entered automatically for you when creating sales orders, purchase orders and invoices etc. You will learn how to monitor stock levels as well as the movement of stock and analyse product transactions using tables, graphs and reports.

Covers

Chapter Six

The Products Toolbar

The Products toolbar provides features for the recording and maintenance of product records and transactions. You have the facility to record the movement of your products and make any adjustments and/or transfer of stock. Product activity can be analysed and reports generated.

Creates a new Product Record.

Opens a Product Record.

To Set up a Price List.

View a Product Activity.

To Run the Product Shortfall Generator.

Make Stock In Adjustments.

Make Stock Out Adjustments.

Record Stock Transfers.

Automatically Make Stock Adjustments.

Check Make-Up Capability For Stock.

For Recording Faulty Stock Returns.

To Produce Product Labels.

To Run Product Reports.

The Product Record

Sage Line 50 allows you to divide products into 999 different categories using the Product Categories option from the Settings menu.

Sage Line 50 allows you to create, edit or delete records for all the products your business sells. Once these records have been set up all you need to do is enter a product code and the details will be automatically included for you on any product invoice, credit note or order you create.

From the Product Record window you can view the sales price and quantity in stock for each product. Use the Products option to:

- Create and maintain records for all products bought and sold.

Opening Balances need setting up for your products following the same procedures as for your customers, suppliers, nominal and bank accounts.

- Record product movements.

- Analyse product transactions using tables or graphs.

- Set up a Bill of Materials.

- Keep track of your stock levels.

From the Product Record window you can view the Sales Price and Quantity in stock for each product, together with the Product Code and Description.

Once a product record has been set up, take care before deleting it, even if there is zero stock and no more is expected. It may still belong to a part allocated order.

1 To bring up the Products window click Products from the Sage Line 50 toolbar.

2 To view Product details, select the product and click Record.

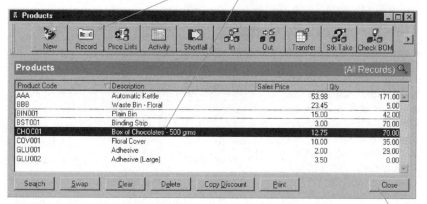

Use the Stock Take option to make adjustments to your stock levels after you have completed a stock take. All you need to do is enter the current stock levels for your products and Sage Line 50 makes all of the necessary adjustments for you.

3 To finish click Close.

You may find it easier at first to let the Product Record Wizard create a new product record for you. Just click on the New option from the Products window.

You can update the sales price for all product items using the Global Changes option from the Tools menu. You can increase or decrease the price by a sum or a percentage.

If the Ignore Stock Levels check box is selected (ticked) on the product record, its details will not appear on some reports, i.e., Stock History.

You can save your stock take details to a file for opening at a later date, to continue with the stock take, or to view the adjustments that you previously made. Remember, however, to enter all of your stock take details before you process any transactions that alter your stock levels. This is because your stock details may change between the date that the last stock date was saved and the next time it is re-opened.

Entering a product record

1 From the Products window click on Record.

2 Type a unique Product Code here and press Tab.

3 Enter Description.

4 Enter relevant details here.

5 Choose a Nominal sales account for this product.

6 Select correct VAT code.

7 Enter Sales Price here.

8 Click on O/B button to bring up the Opening Product Setup box.

9 Check for correct Date.

10 Enter Quantity.

11 Enter Cost Price of Product.

12 Click Save.

13 Enter any remaining details on the Product Record.

14 Click Save to keep the record, or Discard to abort.

15 Click Close to return to Products window.

The In Stock quantity automatically increases when recording an adjustment in a delivery, or posting a credit note for that product. The figure decreases when recording an adjustment out, when a sales order is despatched or when an invoice is posted.

If stock level falls below the re-order level, the item appears red in the Products window and also appears on the Re-order report.

If you do not enter a Cost Price in the Opening Product Setup box, the product cost is recorded as zero. This could affect your finance reports later.

With versions 7 & 8 you can now set up different price lists and allocate different customers to them. You can do this in the Customers screen or by clicking on the Price Lists button on the Products toolbar and doing steps 2–8 on Page 24.

Entering details onto the Product Record

Whilst the Product Record has been designed to accept a considerable amount of detail, not every item is applicable to all products. However, to make reporting more accurate later, you should try and include as much detail as possible about a product when adding records.

Not all of the boxes on the Product Record will accept user entry though. Sage Line 50 calculates or generates the following information and enters it for you. It cannot be directly edited.

Allocated	This figure shows the quantity of the product which has been partly or fully allocated on the sales order, but which has not yet been despatched.
Free Stock	Sage Line 50 calculates the Free Stock as being the In Stock total minus the Allocated stock total.
On Order	Using the Purchase Orders option, this is the quantity of the product which has been put 'on order'.
Last Ord Qty	This shows the amount of stock ordered when the last purchase order for this product was put 'on order'.
Last Ord Date	This shows the date of the last purchase order raised for this product after it had been put on order.
Cost Price	This is the latest cost price for the product item, entered using the Opening Balance option, the Adjustments In option, Purchase Order Processing or the Global Changes option (useful for updating cost prices for all or selected product items).

When running financial or management reports, you must remember that Sage Line 50 will use this latest price even though products already in stock may have actually cost more or less. This may, on occasion, give distorted figures, such as when calculating the total cost value of a product item in stock.

Product Defaults

To save time and make the process of creating new product records easier, Sage Line 50 lets you set up certain product defaults.

Whenever a new product record is created, certain regular details, e.g. Nominal Code, Tax Code, Department etc., are asked for. If you use a recording system where these codes remain the same for most of your products, default settings can be set up which will then appear automatically in each new product record without you having to enter them every time. You set up product defaults as follows:

Use the Departments option from the Settings menu to quickly set up department names.

1 From the Sage Line 50 menu bar, select Settings, then Product Defaults.

2 Enter the Nominal Code to be used by default whenever you create orders and product invoices.

3 Select the VAT rate code from the drop-down list box.

Sage Line 50 stores up to a maximum of six decimal places for rounding up for both product quantity and sales price.

4 Describe the unit of sale here, e.g. 'each', 'box'.

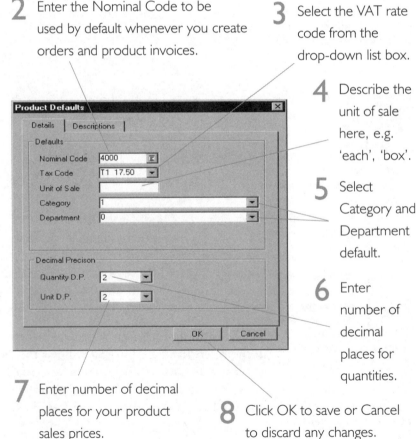

5 Select Category and Department default.

6 Enter number of decimal places for quantities.

If you set the Unit DP to a value greater than 2, the net amount on any product invoice you create will still be rounded to 2 decimal places.

7 Enter number of decimal places for your product sales prices.

8 Click OK to save or Cancel to discard any changes.

Using Search

Using Search speeds up the process of searching for specific product records, for example to show products which match a particular description, or those with a stock level that has fallen below the required re-order level. The following example shows how to set up a search to restrict Product Records to only those with less than 50 in stock:

 Make full use of the drop-down buttons in the right hand corner of each field. These buttons are normally hidden until you click on the field.

1 Click the Search button in the bottom left hand corner of the Products window to bring up the Search window.

 The calculator button is a handy way of making an entry in the Value field.

2 Click here and select Where.

3 Select Quantity in stock in this field.

4 Select Is Less Than here.

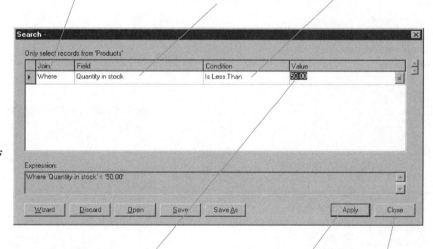

 Use the Save button to record searches you use frequently. You can then recall these as required from the Search window.

5 Enter a value of 50 in this field

6 Click Apply, then Close to return to the Products window.

 Search remains applied to a list until you click the search icon on the right hand side of the title bar:

7 Note that only records matching the search are displayed. The title bar indicates Search is applied.

8 To cancel the search and show all records, click the icon here.

Bill of Materials

Use the Transfer button from the Products window to increase the stock levels of your product assemblies.

This term relates to a product you hold in stock made up from other products you keep. The made up product is sometimes known as a product assembly and is said to have a Bill of Materials. For example, a first aid kit is a product assembly consisting of various components – bandages, tablets, plasters, cream etc.

For businesses selling a product made up of other products, it is useful to set up a Bill of Materials. In Sage Line 50 this feature keeps track of stock levels and can automatically calculate how many products you can make up for sale from the stock you hold and at what cost price. To set up a Bill of Materials for a product do the following:

The Bill of Materials table details each individual component for the product assembly on a separate line. Sage Line 50 allows for a maximum of ten components per product assembly.

1 From the Products window, select the product you wish to set up a Bill of Materials for, then click Record.

2 Click the BOM tab from the Product Record.

3 Enter Product Code for each item.

See how many product assemblies you can make up by using the Calculate button and looking in the Available to Makeup box.

Product Code	Asm	Link	Description	Qty
BIN001	0	1	Plain Bin	1.00
BST001	0	1	Binding Strip	2.00
COV001	0	1	Floral Cover	1.00
GLU001	0	1	Adhesive	1.00

Assembly Level 1   Link Level 0   Available to Makeup 35.00   Calculate

Save   Discard   Delete   Back   Next   Close

4 Enter quantity required for product assembly.

Use the Finder button to quickly locate Product Codes.

6 Click Save to store Bill of Materials, or Discard to start again.

5 Click Calculate to see how many you can make.

7 Click Close.

Viewing Transactions

To amend values for all, or a selected group of products within the Product Record, select the Global Changes option from the Tools menu.

The Sales Tab

You can use this dialog box to view the sales value and quantity sold for your selected product during the financial year on a month by month basis. With a record selected:

1 From the Product Record click on the Sales tab.

2 Use scroll bar to view different months.

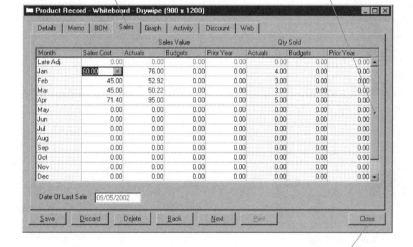

3 Click Close.

Use Copy Matrix button to copy discount structure from another discounted product.

Use a range of 2D and 3D chart types to compare how you did last year with this year's budget.

Product Discounts

1 From the Product Record click on the Discount tab.

2 Enter quantity for customer to qualify for a discount.

3 Enter % Discount.

4 Discounted value is calculated for you.

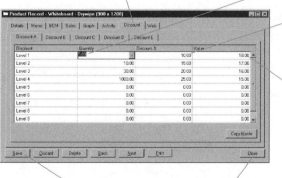

Sage Line 50 provides you with five different methods of discounting sales to your Customers.

5 Repeat as required.

6 Click Save to store entries, then Close.

Product Activity

To print a report of your product activity, use the Reports option from the Products window and run the activity layout.

Details regarding adjustments of goods in and out, stock transfers, current quantities in stock, on order and allocated prove invaluable when trying to fulfil orders or analyse and track the movement of stock.

You can decide when you no longer wish to retain certain transactions on your system by using the Clear Stock option. This facility enables transactions to be cleared from your Product History prior to a specific date.

Where activities have been cleared at the month end, they will be shown as carried forward totals with a Ref. of O/BAL, usually at the top of the list.

It is important that you understand the following terms when trying to calculate the availability of stock and to understand the product reports produced by Sage Line 50:

Tp: A code to identify the type of transaction, where:

AI	=	Adjustment In.
AO	=	Adjustment Out.
MI	=	Movement In (product transfer only).
MO	=	Movement Out (product transfers only).
GR	=	Goods Returned (via credit notes).
GO	=	Goods Out (via sales orders and product invoices).
GI	=	Goods In (via purchase orders).
DI	=	Damages In.
DO	=	Damages Out.

To clear stock transactions, choose the Period End option from the Tools menu and click the Clear Stock option. Adjustments made are brought forward as opening balances, showing quantities used, in AI and MI.

Use the type code WO for recording faulty goods as write-offs.

Used: This is the sum of all the AO (Adjustments Out), GO (Goods Out) and MO (Movements Out) quantities for the product within the specified date range.

To record faulty products use the Returns button from the Products toolbar. Use Sage Help for more information on recording faulty stock.

Cost: If the transaction line refers to an AI (Adjustment In), GI (Goods In), GR (Goods Returned) or MI (Movement In), this shows the cost price.

Sale: Where a transaction line refers to an AO (Adjustment Out), GO (Goods Out) or GR (Goods Returned), this shows the sales price.

Viewing a product's activity is also available using the Activity tab from the Product Record window.

Qty on Order: This is the product quantity which has been ordered and placed on order using the Purchase Order option, but not yet delivered.

Qty Allocated: This shows the product quantity that has been Allocated to sales orders using the Sales Order Processing option.

Qty in Stock: This is the sum of all the AI (Adjustments In), MI (Movements In), GI (Goods In) and GR (Goods Received), less the quantity used for the specified period.

Unless you change the default date range, all product activity will be displayed.

Qty Available: The Quantity in Stock less Quantity Allocated.

To view Activity from the Products window:

1 Click on the product or products required.

2 Click on Activity to bring up the Date Range box.

Use the Finder button to select another Product Code if required.

3 Enter From and To date.

4 Click OK.

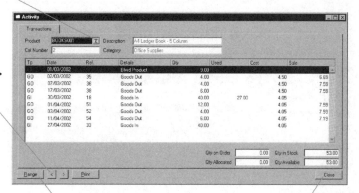

Use the < and > buttons to move between selected products.

5 Click Range to enter new Date Range.

6 Click Close when finished.

Product Adjustments

If there is a discrepancy after a stock take, enter the stock adjustment using the Stock Take option.

The In and Out options from the Product window are used to record adjustments to your product's stock levels, such as when stock is received into stores, an order is returned, or stock is taken out as a damaged.

The In button is used to enter any increase in a product's available stock, whilst the Out option is for recording a decrease.

To make Adjustments In

Cost prices are important to the valuation of the stock as product levels are controlled on a first in, first out basis. Always enter cost prices, therefore, to achieve accurate valuation reporting.

1 From the Products window click the In option.

2 Enter Product Code.

3 Enter quantity in.

4 Enter Date & Ref.

5 Enter Cost.

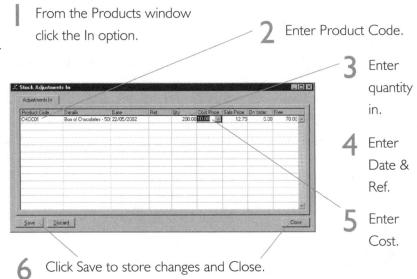

Use the Goods Received Note number as a Reference.

6 Click Save to store changes and Close.

The Out button is used to record any miscellaneous product movements which decrease a product's available stock level and where no product invoice has been raised.

You cannot use the Returns option for non-stock or service items.

To make Adjustments Out

1 Click the Out option.

2 Enter Product Code.

3 Enter quantity and click Save and Close.

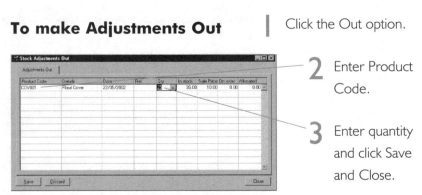

Product Transfers

You can only use a product code which has been previously set up to be a product assembly using the BOM option.

This feature is used for increasing the In Stock quantity of Product Assemblies using components currently in stock. The Product Assemblies are set up using the Bill of Materials option (see page 80).

Use the Calendar if you need to make a quick date change.

When using the Product Transfer option the cost price for each Product Assembly is calculated for you by Sage Line 50, by adding together the cost price of each component.

To make a product transfer from the Products window:

1   Click on the Transfer button.

If you do not have sufficient stock of components to make up the quantity you have entered, Sage Line 50 will display a warning.

2   Click on the Product Code Finder button.

      4   Click OK.

3   Select Product Assembly Code.

New to Sage Line 50 v8, click on the Shortfall button on the Products toolbar to bring up the Shortfall Generator window (Accountant Plus and Financial Controller only). You can now check stock levels and print a report.

Shortfall

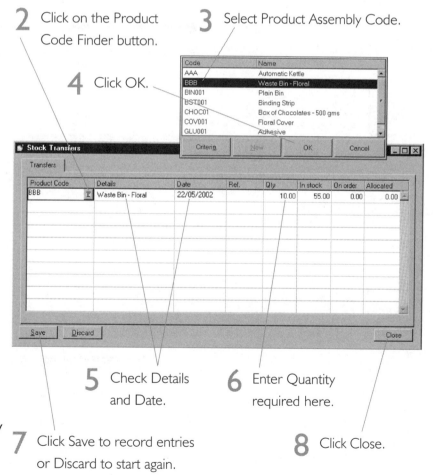

Use Check BOM to quickly check which stock items and components are needed to complete orders.

5   Check Details and Date.

6   Enter Quantity required here.

7   Click Save to record entries or Discard to start again.

8   Click Close.

Product Reports

The Product Reports option allows you to print out a wide range of useful pre-prepared product related reports. These reports show such things as product details and movements, and will help you to keep track of what your company has in stock, its financial value etc.

Additional product reports tailored to your business needs can be created using the Report Designer (See Chapter Twelve). To run a Product Report:

Use the Criteria button on the Products window when you need to select specific ranges of products to report on.

Use the Product Audit Trail to quickly track the movement of stock.

If you selected to print the report, the Windows Print dialog box appears. Use this to select which pages to print and to change your printer settings if necessary.

You can easily generate labels for your products by clicking on the Labels button from the Products toolbar.

1 From the Products window click Reports to bring up the Product Reports list.

2 Click on the report you require.

3 Ensure Preview is selected.

4 Click Run to bring up the Criteria window.

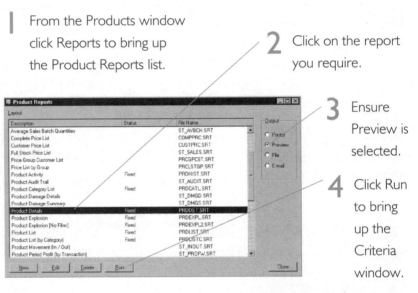

5 Enter Criteria required for report.

6 Click OK to generate report.

7 Click Print, then OK and Close.

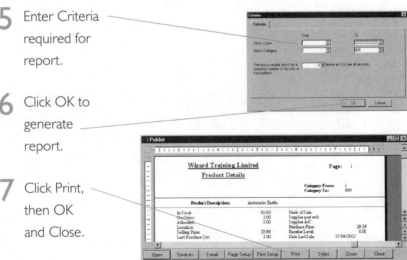

Invoices

This chapter shows you how to produce invoices and credit notes for your products and services. Customers, Products and Nominal Accounts are directly linked to Invoicing so the invoices produced automatically update the relevant ledgers. Any raised invoices not posted or printed can be monitored. Quotes and Proformas can also be generated.

Covers

Chapter Seven

The Invoicing Toolbar

This toolbar provides facilities for generating invoices, quotes, proformas and credit notes for the goods you sell and the services you provide. Ledgers can be automatically updated, transactions printed out and reports generated for analysis purposes.

 To Create or View an Invoice, Pro-forma, Quote or Credit Note.

 To Print an Invoice or Credit Note.

 To Update your Ledgers.

 To Print Invoice Labels.

 To Run Invoicing Reports.

Invoicing

Sage Line 50 generates invoice numbers in sequence, normally starting at 1. However, you can start with your own numbering system, of up to seven digits. This will be incremented for you each time a new invoice is generated.

As you create invoices they are displayed on the Invoicing list box, one line per invoice. This list also includes any product invoices you created using the Sales Order Processing option.

New to Sage Line 50 v8, there is only one New/Edit button on the Invoice toolbar, the type of Invoice or Credit Note is now selected in the Type and Format boxes on the Invoice window.

Invoices remain in the Invoicing window list box until removed using the Delete option.

Processing manually generated invoices, or batch invoicing, i.e., items not generated using Sage Line 50, has already been referred to in Chapters Two and Three. Briefly, Chapter Two (Customers) explains how to log invoices and credit notes within the system after they have been produced and sent to customers. Chapter Three (Suppliers) explains how to record the invoices and credit notes you receive from your suppliers.

Invoicing deals with Sage Line 50 generated invoices, of which there are two basic types. Firstly there is the Product Invoice, which is used for invoicing customers for the products you sell. Each line of the invoice can be used for recording specific product items. Early discount settlement can be offered on these invoices and carriage charges applied.

Meanwhile the Service Invoice is used to invoice customers you have provided a service for. An unlimited amount of text can be entered into the invoice describing the services supplied. Discount settlement can be applied and carriage charges recorded.

Because Sage Line 50 generates these invoices, all the relevant details are automatically recorded and posted for you when you are ready. For invoices where the same information is entered regularly, the Memorise option saves the invoice as a template. This template can then be recalled when required and updated with the new information, saving valuable time.

Also within Invoicing is the facility to generate credit notes for your customers, where products or services for example, have not been received or had to be returned. When these transactions are posted, the ledgers will be updated automatically.

You do, of course, need to keep track of your invoicing. Use the report facility regularly to print out a list of Invoices not yet printed or posted, or to check on stock requirements or shortfalls for the invoices you have generated using this Invoicing option.

Prior to Sage Line 50 v8 the Invoicing toolbar contained separate buttons for Product and Service Invoices and Credit Notes. In version 8, the toolbar contains only one New/Edit button. The type of Invoice or Credit Note is then selected from the Type and Format boxes in the Invoice window.

The Product Invoice

To retrieve and edit an existing invoice, simply select the invoice from the Invoicing window and click New/Edit.

You cannot amend a product invoice where the quantity was entered using the Sales Order Processing option.

New in Sage Line 50 v8, provided the appropriate cost details have been entered on the Product records, use the Profit button to calculate how much profit an Invoice makes.

As well as normal product codes, you can also enter special non-product codes:

S1 = Special product item with price and VAT amount.

S2 = Special product item, exempt for VAT (Tax code T0).

S3 = Special service item with price and VAT amount.

M = Message, with a description and up to two comment lines.

To invoice your customers for the products you sell, use the New/Edit option from the Invoicing toolbar, then select the Product option in the drop down list in the Type box (prior to version 8, click on the Product button on the toolbar). To create an Invoice click Invoicing on the main toolbar, then do the following:

1 Click New/Edit on the Invoicing toolbar. Invoice and Product appears here.

2 Enter the tax point date if different here.

3 Type Sales Order No. if applicable.

4 Enter Customer Account Code.

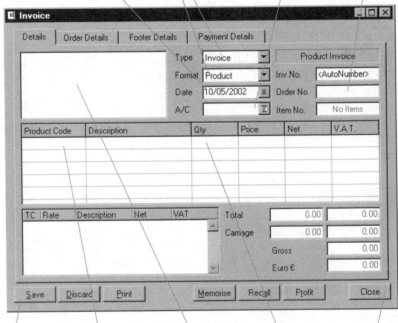

5 Customer details appear here.

6 Enter the Product Code here (use Finder button).

7 Enter Quantity here.

8 Repeat Steps 6 & 7 for further products, then click Save to finish.

9 Click Close.

...cont'd

Product Invoice Order Details

You can record useful additional Order Details on your Invoice if necessary:

1 Click on Order Details tab.

2 Enter Delivery Address.

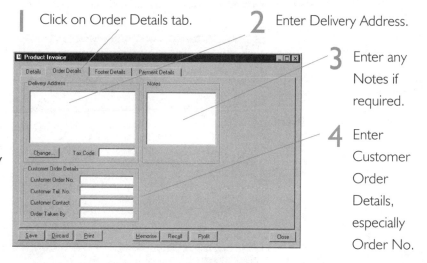

3 Enter any Notes if required.

4 Enter Customer Order Details, especially Order No.

Product Invoice Footer Details

Further details, such as Carriage and Settlement Terms, go in the Footer Details:

5 Click on Footer Details tab.

6 Enter any Carriage details here.

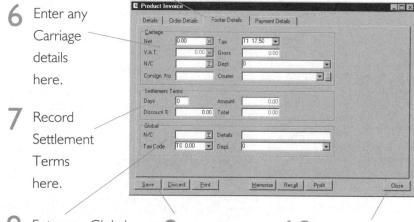

7 Record Settlement Terms here.

8 Enter any Global detail changes.

9 Click Save.

10 Click Close to finish.

Printing an Invoice

When using the Invoicing option to create invoices and credit notes, you can choose either to *print straight away or save them as a batch for printing later using the Print option on the Invoicing Toolbar.*

Sage Line 50 gives you the option to print Invoices or Credit Notes either immediately, or at a later date. To print straight away after you have entered all of the details, instead of clicking Save (the Invoice is automatically saved in version 8) do the following:

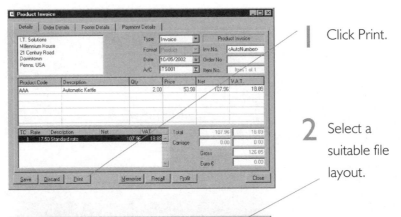

1 Click Print.

2 Select a suitable file layout.

Batching invoices or credit notes is useful if you only have one printer. You simply load the correct stationery in the printer once, then print them all in one go.

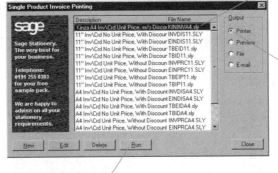

3 Check Output is set to Printer.

4 Click Run.

5 Click OK to print.

If no records are selected from the list in the Invoicing window, all non-printed invoices or credit notes will be printed.

6 Select Preview then click OK.

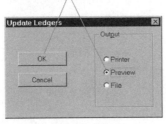

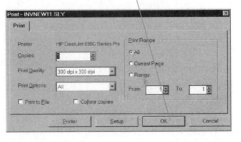

7 Click Close to finish.

The Service Invoice

To avoid having to re-create the same invoice details all the time, store a template using the Memorise button.

To invoice customers for the services you provide instead of products you sell, you should generate a Service Invoice, still using the New/Edit button from the Invoicing Toolbar. An unlimited amount of text can be entered to describe the services provided, and each service can be analysed to a different nominal account. Settlement discounts can also be applied as well as recording carriage charges.

Sage Line 50 warns you if a selected customer account has been marked as 'on hold' on the Customer Record.

As with Product Invoices, a Service Invoice can be saved to print in a batch later or printed straight away. At this point you have the option to update the ledgers at the same time or leave them until a more appropriate time.

Always select the Invoice Format BEFORE entering details.

1 Click New/Edit from the Invoicing toolbar and select Service here.

2 Change date if different.

3 Enter Order Number.

4 Enter Customer Code.

Select a service item and click on the Edit box or Press F3 to view item details. If required, you can alter the Posting Details or enter a Job Reference.

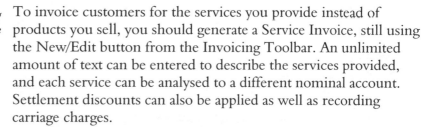

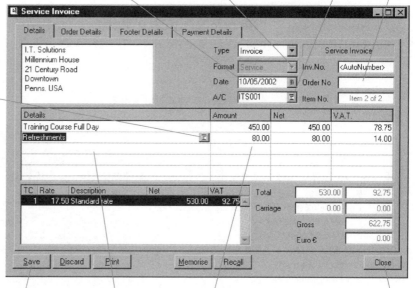

If you make a mistake, simply click Discard and start again.

5 Type service Details here.

6 Enter net Price.

7 Repeat Steps 5 & 6 as required.

8 Click Save to print later, or Print to print now.

9 Click Close to finish.

Service Invoice Order Details

You can record useful additional Order Details on your Service Invoice if required:

Any changes made to the delivery details are not saved back to the Customer Record.

1 Click on Order Details tab.

2 Enter Delivery Address.

3 Enter any Notes if required.

4 Enter Customer Order Details, such as Order No.

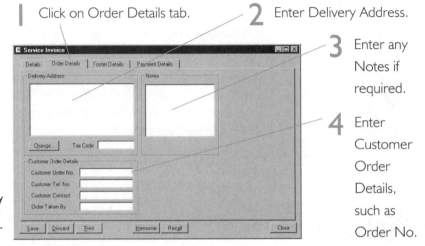

Using the Footer Details tab you can enter or amend any settlement terms you operate with your customer. You can also add any analysis conditions that you wish to apply to the entire invoice.

Service Invoice Footer Details

You can record details such as Carriage and Settlement Terms in the Footer Details box:

5 Click on Footer Details tab.

6 Enter any Carriage details here.

For payments you have received which can be allocated against the invoice, record the details using the Payment Details tab.

7 Record Settlement Terms here.

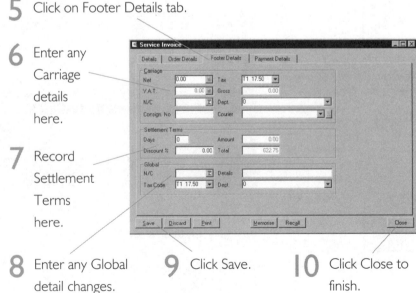

8 Enter any Global detail changes.

9 Click Save.

10 Click Close to finish.

The Skeleton Invoice

Any unwanted skeleton invoices can be deleted using the Edit menu (recall option).

For information that is regularly repeated when creating an invoice, use the Memorise option to store the invoice as a template. You can then recall this template as and when required, and update it with the new information, thus saving valuable time and reduce keying errors.

This facility is available for both Product and Service Invoices, as well as the Product and Service Credit Notes.

When you load your skeleton, all the details that you saved appear automatically.

1 On the Details screen enter regularly used details only, such as Customer A/C Ref. and item Details. Omit the Price.

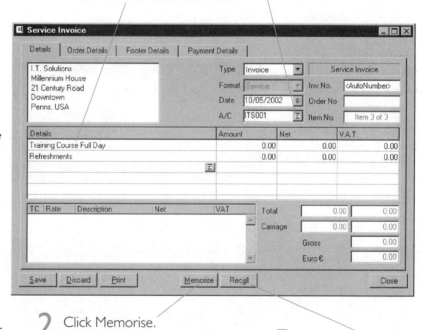

A Product Invoice uses the non-product code S3 for a service item.

A quick way to alter the date in a Date box is to use the up or down cursor keys to move through the days. Pressing Page Up or Page Down moves through the months.

2 Click Memorise.

3 Enter Filename and Description.

4 Click Save.

5 When you need to use a layout, click Recall.

6 Select your layout from the list.

7 Click Load.

Product Credit Note

From time to time goods sent to customers may be returned as faulty, past an expiry date etc., or the customer may simply have been overcharged by mistake.

Instead of correcting the original invoice, a Product Credit Note can be issued to the Customer, detailing the amount owing to them. When your ledgers are updated, the necessary postings will be made to reflect this amendment. Do the following to create a Product Credit Note:

A VAT only credit note can be raised where a customer has been invoiced and charged tax for goods which are exempt from VAT.

From Sage Line 50 v8, you must select the Invoice Format, i.e., Product or Service, prior to entering any product or service details. Once you begin to enter these details, the Format box goes to grey and can only be changed by discarding the Invoice and starting again.

One-off details can be entered against each Credit Note product item to record, for example, changes to customer discounts, address, unit price or simply to add a short comment.

1 Click New/Edit from the Invoicing toolbar and select Credit here.

2 Change date if different.

3 Enter Order Number.

4 Enter Customer Code.

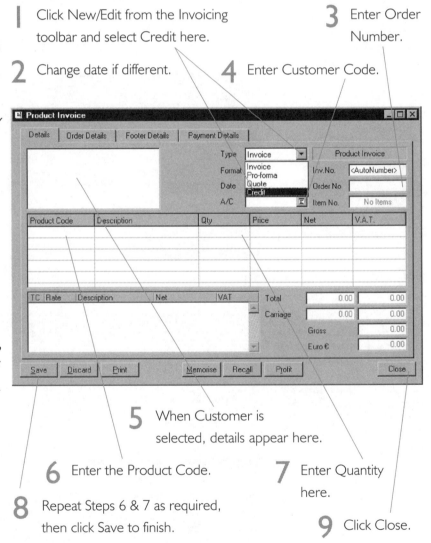

5 When Customer is selected, details appear here.

6 Enter the Product Code.

7 Enter Quantity here.

8 Repeat Steps 6 & 7 as required, then click Save to finish.

9 Click Close.

Service Credit Note

A Service Credit Note can be used where, for example, customers have been charged or overcharged for a service they have not received. In this case you would issue a Service Credit Note detailing the changes made and the amount owing to the customer. When the ledgers are updated, the necessary postings will be made.

This method replaces editing the original service invoice and regenerating a new one:

 If you have a standard type of Credit Note that you use regularly, create a template for it and save it using the Memorise button. You can then recall this template as and when necessary.

1 Click New/Edit from the Invoicing toolbar and select Credit and Service here.

2 Enter date for the Credit Note if different.

3 Enter Order Number.

4 Enter Customer Code.

 To edit an existing credit note, enter the credit note number in the Credit No. box and press TAB.

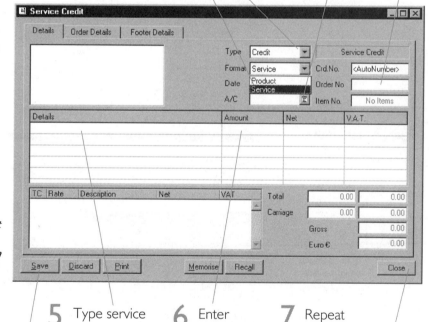

 Choosing the Save button saves the credit note for printing later in a 'batch'. To print the credit note straight away and update the ledgers, choose the Print button instead.

5 Type service credit Details here.

6 Enter Amount of refund.

7 Repeat Steps 5 & 6 as required.

8 Click Save to print later, or Print to print now.

9 Click Close to finish.

Updating your Ledgers

By regularly updating your stock records, you may find you now have enough free stock to complete outstanding sales orders.

After creating your invoices and credit notes, the Update function is used to transfer details to the customer and nominal ledgers and, if appropriate, to amend product records.

Sage Line 50 gives you the option to print the update report immediately, preview it first so that you can select only certain pages for printing, or to save the report as a file. To perform an Update, do the following:

1 From the Invoicing window select the invoices and credit notes for updating.

2 Click Update to display the Output options.

After Updating, you can view the changes to the customer ledger and stock by using the Activity option.

Use the Clear button to deselect all before starting.

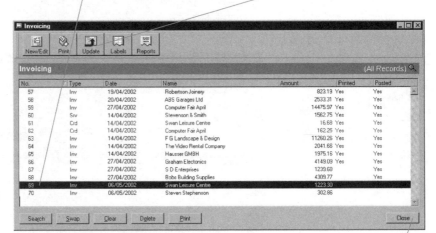

Always make sure you select at least one Invoice or Credit Note before using the Update function otherwise Sage Line 50 will ask you if you want to process ALL non-posted invoices and credit notes.

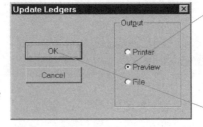

3 In the Output box click Preview.

4 Click OK to generate the update.

5 On the report, click Print to bring up the Windows Print dialog box, then click OK to print.

6 Click Close to return to the Invoicing window, then Close again.

Printing for Batch Invoicing

You can reprint your invoices as many times as you wish.

When you created Invoices or Credit Notes, both Product or Service, you may have decided to leave printing them until later as a batch. This can often save time when setting up file layouts and having to change the printer stationery.

For example, you may have created two Service invoices which now need printing. You would do the following:

Use the Search button if you wish to print a number of invoices or credit notes that match a particular condition.

1 From the Invoicing window, select the invoices for printing.

2 Click on the Print icon.

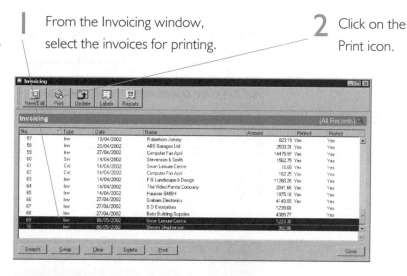

Select the correct layout file for printing your invoice or credit notes, depending upon which type of printer and paper size you are using.

3 Ensure Preview is selected.

4 Select Layout required.

5 Click Run.

Standard layouts can be edited or new layouts created where necessary.

7 On the preview, click Print to bring up the Windows Print dialog box, then click OK to print.

6 Click Yes to confirm layout.

8 Click Close to return to the Invoicing window.

Producing Reports

The Reports option allows you to produce a wide range of reports about your product and service invoices, as well as your credit notes. Use these reports regularly to keep your business up to date. To print an invoice report:

Save time: instead of searching through all your invoices for those not yet posted, use the Invoices Not Posted report.

1 Click Reports from the Invoicing toolbar.

2 Select report required.

3 Ensure Preview is selected.

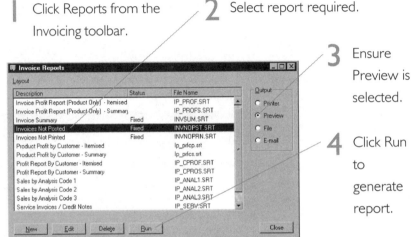

Use the Invoices Not Printed report regularly to keep up to date with sending out Invoices.

4 Click Run to generate report.

Alternatively, use the Search button on the Invoicing window to only list invoices not yet printed, posted, product only or service only etc.

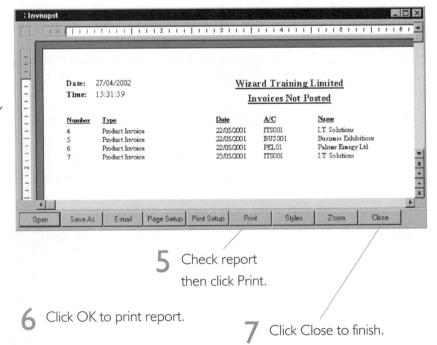

Use the Labels button from the Invoicing toolbar to quickly print out invoice address labels.

5 Check report then click Print.

6 Click OK to print report.

7 Click Close to finish.

Processing Sales Orders

This chapter shows you how to keep track of your Sales Orders. You will learn how to allocate and despatch stock to these orders to keep your stock levels up-to-date. You will be shown how to automatically generate a Sales Invoice for each despatch you make and how to print Sales Orders, Delivery Notes and a variety of reports.

Covers

Chapter Eight

The Sales Order Processing Toolbar

The SOP toolbar provides a number of features for creating a sales order and then controlling the allocation of stock to that order. Once you are ready to deliver the stock, you can despatch it and Sage Line 50 will automatically handle the stock record updates. From this toolbar you can also print sales orders, whilst information regarding sales order processing can be easily obtained by using the various report layouts already provided for you.

 To Create or View a Sales Order.

 To Allocate Stock to a Sales Order.

 To Despatch a Sales Order.

 To Make Changes to a Sales Order.

 To Run the ShortFall Generator.

 To Print Sales Orders.

 To Print Sales Order Labels.

 To Run Sales Order Reports.

The Sales Order

On a Network, if a number of users create Sales Orders at the same time and one order is abandoned, the order numbers will no longer run consecutively because the abandoned number will not be used.

Sales orders can be created for the products you supply and sent to customers by using the Enter option from the Sales Order Processing toolbar. Details from your Product records are automatically entered onto the Sales Orders whilst extra details can also be added, such as a delivery address, a customer order number for future reference or a settlement discount etc.

To create a Sales Order, click SOP from the Sage Line 50 toolbar, then do the following:

1 Click Enter from the Sales Order Processing toolbar.

2 Type required date if different to current date.

4 Customer details appear here.

3 Enter Customer Account Code.

Use the Message box (i.e., the product code M) to add any text to the main body of the sales order, for example, 'goods supplied free'.

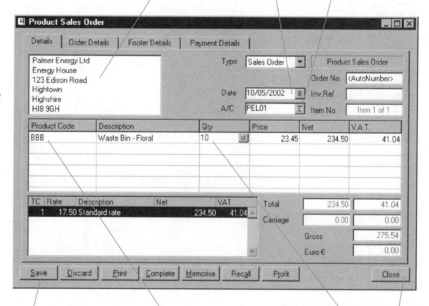

To include special one-off details against a sales item, click the Edit button from the Description box.

5 Enter the Product Code here (use Finder button).

6 Enter Quantity ordered here.

7 Repeat Steps 5 & 6 for additional products, then if finished click Save.

8 Click Close.

Each line of the Sales Order is treated separately for product discount purposes. Make sure you only enter each product code once if a customer qualifies for a product discount.

Sales Order Details

On the previous page you were shown how to create a Sales Order and save it immediately if no further details needed entering. Sage Line 50, however, gives you the option to enter additional details about the order, such as where it should be delivered if different from the main address etc.

From the Sales Order window, do the following to enter additional order details:

1 Click on the Order Details tab.

2 Enter Delivery Address (not yet set up) if required.

3 Record any Notes here.

Once a Sales Order has been despatched in part or full, you cannot decrease the quantity of any product ordered to less than the quantity despatched.

Product Sales Order

Details | Order Details | Footer Details | Payment Details

Delivery Address

Change...   Tax Code:

Notes

Customer Order Details

Customer Order No.

Customer Tel. No. 01987 345345

Customer Contact Alan Volt

Order Taken By

Sales Order Status

Allocation

Despatch

Due / /

Save | Discard | Print | Complete | Memorise | Recall | Profit | Close

Sage Line 50 will generate an invoice and enter the Invoice Number for you automatically when the order is Despatched.

4 Enter any relevant Customer Order Details, such as a Customer Order Number.

5 You may wish to enter Due Despatch date here.

6 Click Save when finished.

7 Click Close.

Allocating Stock

Once a Sales Order has been created, stock needs allocating to it before any despatches can be recorded for the Order. Using the Allocate option from the Sales Order Processing toolbar automatically allocates the necessary stock needed for the selected Sales Order.

Sometimes there is insufficient stock available to complete an Order, in which case the Order will be marked as 'Part' complete. There may be times when you have enough stock, but wish to only send part of the Order. In this case you would use the Amend option to make changes to the Order. To allocate batched Sales Orders, do the following from within the Sales Order Processing window:

1 Click on the Sales Orders you wish to Allocate.

2 Click Allocate.

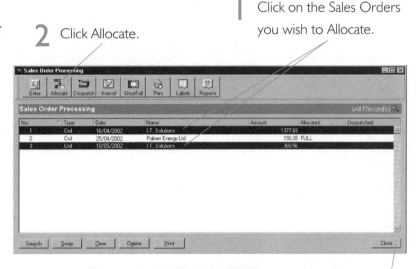

3 Click Yes to Confirm Allocation of stock.

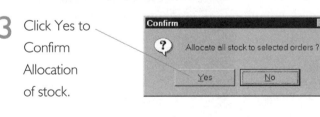

4 Note change in Sales Order Status.

5 Click Close.

Despatching Sales Orders

To Despatch a batch of Sales Orders, select the required Sales Orders by clicking on them to highlight, or use the Swap and Clear buttons.

Once stock is allocated to your sales orders, it can be despatched at any time. The Despatch option also updates the product records and creates a Product Invoice for the order, as well as printing a Delivery Note.

The product invoices created through Sales Order Processing appears in the Invoicing window. These invoices can be edited, but you cannot change the quantity of the product despatched. They can then be printed and posted to the sales and nominal ledgers in the same manner as invoices created using the Invoicing option.

If only part of an order is despatched, Sage Line 50 creates an invoice for that part. This means that when the order is fully despatched, there will be more than one invoice for it.

1 From the Sales Order Processing window, select the required Sales Orders.

2 Click Despatch.

3 Click Yes to print Delivery Notes if required.

Click the Complete button from the Sales Order window to automatically save the order, Allocate stock to it and record the Despatch all in one go.

4 Select Delivery Note layout.

5 Click Run.

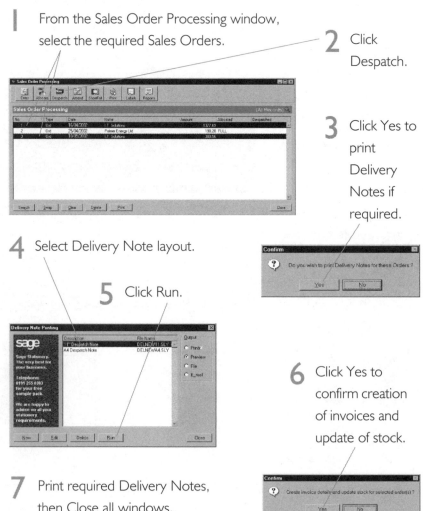

6 Click Yes to confirm creation of invoices and update of stock.

Use the Shortfall option new to Sage Line 50 versions 7 & 8 to see if you have enough stock to fulfil orders and to place purchase orders if you do not.

7 Print required Delivery Notes, then Close all windows.

Amending & Printing Sales Orders

When you Amend the allocation of stock to a sales order, the allocated status of the order in the Sales Orders window may change to either Full, Part or no status at all.

If you have allocated stock to a sales order, but have not yet despatched all of it, you can amend this allocation. This allows you to despatch a full order by reducing the stock allocation of another customer's order, hence perhaps reducing the number of customers waiting.

To amend the allocation of stock on a sales order

With Line 50 versions 7 & 8 you can now raise an invoice even if you have negative stock.

1 Select the Order from the Sales Order Processing window and click Amend.

2 Amend the Allocation.

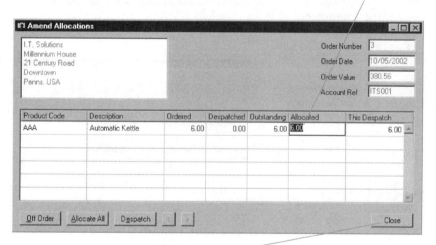

By batching your orders, you can print them all out together after setting up the printer with the correct sales order stationery.

3 Click Close and note any change in Status.

Printing Batched Orders

Always Preview anything to be printed out to save wasting paper.

1 Select orders for printing from Sales Order Processing window and Click Print.

Save time by sending your Sales Orders using e-mail.

2 Select layout required.

3 Click Run.

4 Click Print, then Close.

Sales Orders Reports

Sage Line 50 provides you with a large variety of reports to help you run the Sales Order side of your business. For example, you have the facility to print a picking list for your warehouse from a particular order or the sales order shortage report to show you any shortfalls in the stock.

These reports are generated from the information entered when you created a sales order. To generate, for example, a Sales Order Picking List:

Regularly use the Sales Orders to be Invoiced report to keep up to date with your invoicing.

The number of sales orders included in your reports can be restricted by using the Search button on the Sales Orders window.

To check how many despatched orders have gone out for a particular time period, use the Despatched Sales Orders report and apply the Order Date Criteria.

Use the Labels button from the Sales Order toolbar to quickly print out Sales Order Address or Stock labels.

1 From the Sales Order Processing window, click Reports.

2 Select required Layout.

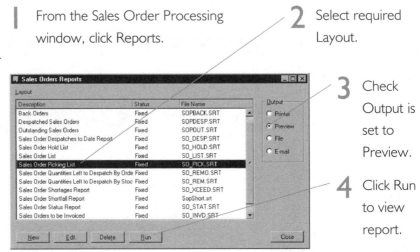

3 Check Output is set to Preview.

4 Click Run to view report.

5 Enter Criteria i.e. Sales Order number.

6 Click OK to generate report.

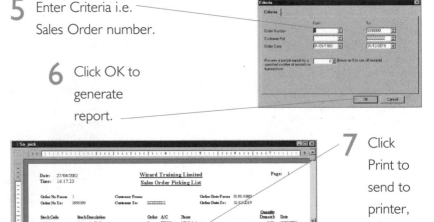

7 Click Print to send to printer, then OK & Close.

Purchase Orders

In this chapter you will learn how to create and print Purchase Orders to send to your suppliers. You will be shown how to monitor orders raised and record deliveries received as well as produce reports to help you keep track of your Purchase Orders.

Covers

Chapter Nine

Purchase Order Processing Toolbar

From the POP toolbar you can create and print Purchase Orders as well as make amendments to orders you have already created. You have facilities for recording deliveries and producing useful reports about your Purchase Orders, such as which have been delivered in part or full, or which are still outstanding.

 To Create or View a Purchase Order.

 To Put a Purchase Order 'on order'.

 To Record Purchase Order Deliveries.

 To Complete a Goods Received Note.

 To Make Changes to a Purchase Order.

 To Automatically Update the Purchase Ledger.

 To Print a Purchase Order.

 To Print Purchase Order Labels.

 To Run Purchase Order Reports.

Creating a Purchase Order

To edit an existing order simply double-click on it in the Purchase Order Processing window.

To record order details of any products you buy from a supplier, use the Enter option from the Purchase Order toolbar. Details entered straight onto the Purchase Order screen are taken directly from the product records for you by Sage Line 50.

You can also include additional details, such as delivery address or any settlement discount given to you by your supplier, to the order. To create a Purchase Order click POP from the Sage Line 50 toolbar then follow these steps:

You can increase, but not decrease, the quantity for any Purchase Order you have already despatched in full or part.

1 Click Enter from the Purchase Orders Processing toolbar.

2 Check required date is entered here.

4 Supplier details appear here.

3 Enter Supplier Account Code.

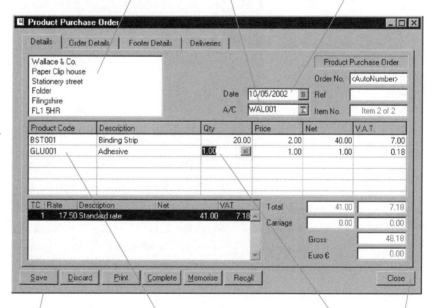

On a network, if two users create a Purchase Order at the same time and one of the orders is abandoned, the abandoned number will not be re-used, so numbers will not run consecutively.

Use the product code M for non-payment products.

5 Enter the Product Code here (use Finder button).

6 Enter Quantity being ordered.

7 Repeat Steps 5 & 6 for additional products, click Save when finished.

8 Click Close.

If you enter an Account Code that is not already set up, Sage Line 50 automatically invokes the Finder so you can choose another account or create a new one using the New button.

Entering Purchase Order Details

You may need to record further details on your Purchase Order, such as delivery details, carriage costs, settlement terms, supplier contact or the name of the person who took your order.

Sage Line 50 lets you do this through the Order Details or Footer Details tabs. From the Purchase Order window, do the following to enter additional order details:

1 Click on the Order Details tab.

2 Enter Delivery Address here if required.

3 Record any Notes you wish to add here.

Save your Purchase Order as a Skeleton if you use these details regularly.

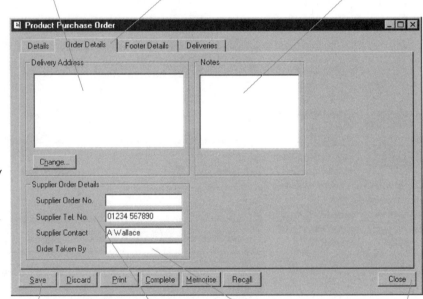

If you have already received the products for this Purchase Order, choose the Complete button.

Use the Footer Details tab to record any Carriage or Settlement terms and the Deliveries tab to view delivery information.

4 Enter any relevant Supplier Order Details, such as an Order or Telephone Number.

5 You can change who took the order here.

6 Click Save when all details have been entered.

7 Click Close.

Placing Purchase Orders 'on order'

Once a Purchase Order has been created, it has to be placed 'on order' before any deliveries can be recorded for it. Sage Line 50 then updates each product record with the new order details accordingly.

Use the Order option to automatically place a single or batch of Purchase Orders 'on order', as follows:

Click the Search button to set up a filter to list only the orders you wish to work with.

To avoid costly mistakes, always check that the status of an order shows ON-ORDER after going through the process of placing it on order.

To remove a Purchase Order simply highlight it and click on the Delete button.

You can also put Purchase Orders 'on order' from within the Amend Deliveries option.

I From the Purchase Order Processing window, highlight all the orders you wish to place 'on order' by clicking on them.

2 Click Order.

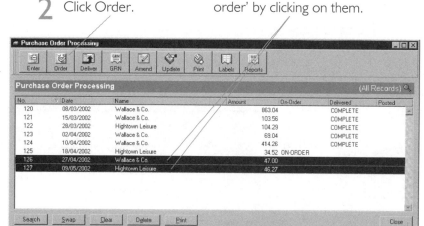

3 Click Yes to Confirm you wish to place the selected items 'on order'.

Confirm

(?) Place all selected items On-Order ?

[Yes]   [No]

4 Click No here to print a copy of the Purchase Order later, else Yes to print now.

Confirm

(?) Do you want to print the Purchase Orders for the selected items ?

[Yes]   [No]

5 Note that items are now ON-ORDER.

6 Click Close.

Recording Deliveries

You can only record deliveries for orders which you have already put 'on order'.

To automatically record the complete delivery of stock for Purchase Orders use the Deliver option from the Purchase Order Processing toolbar.

You should remember that Sage Line 50 always assumes that you have taken full delivery of all the products needed to complete the selected Purchase Order. If a part delivery needs recording, you must record the delivery using the Amend function (see page 116).

To record Purchase Order deliveries do the following:

Sage Line 50 automatically makes adjustments for each product that you mark as delivered.

1 From the Purchase Order Processing window select any orders you wish to mark as Delivered.

2 Click Deliver.

When delivery is recorded for selected Purchase Orders, the Delivered status shows Complete.

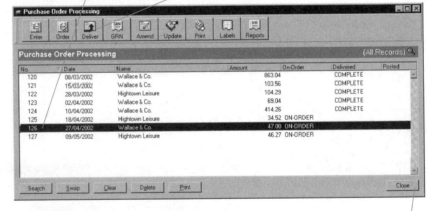

When you use the Delivery option it is assumed that you have taken full delivery of all items on the Purchase Order. The Delivery record cannot be altered later.

4 Note the Purchase Order now displays as COMPLETE.

3 Click Yes in this box to Confirm delivery and update stock records.

5 If finished, Click Close.

Processing Purchases Manually

Use the < and > buttons to move between selected Purchase Orders.

To check and keep track of your Purchase Orders use the Amend option. In this window you can manually place them 'on order' (thus updating On Order levels for appropriate product records), record full or part deliveries of stock against each order and cancel orders.

Placing a Purchase Order 'on order' manually

You have already learned how to place Purchase Orders 'on order' using the Order button (Page 113). However, Sage Line 50 also allows you to do this manually as follows:

1 From Purchase Order Processing window, select the purchase order you require.

2 Click Amend to bring up the Amend Deliveries window.

You can cancel a Purchase Order which is 'on order' with the Amend option. Just click Off Order to mark it as cancelled or click Order to put it back 'on order'.

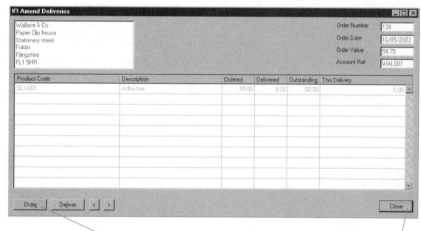

Cancelling an order does not affect any part deliveries which may have been previously recorded for that Purchase Order.

3 Click on the Order button to place 'on order'.

4 Note the order now looks normal and the full order quantity appears in This Delivery.

5 Click Close.

Recording Deliveries Manually

You use the Deliver button from the Purchase Order Processing toolbar only when you have received full delivery of an order.

If the order is not 'on order' or has been cancelled, Sage Line 50 will remind you to place the Purchase Order 'on order' to enable you to record the delivery.

If you wish to record part deliveries, then you must use the Amend option, though you can still record full deliveries this way as well, should you need to. To record a Purchase Order part delivery, follow these steps:

1 From the Purchase Order Processing window select the order you wish to record a delivery for.

2 Click Amend.

Use the Amend option if you wish to record part deliveries for your Purchase Orders.

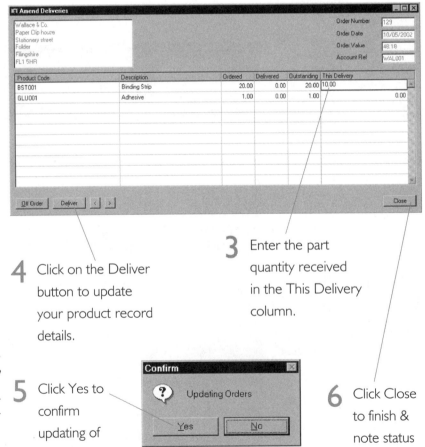

The Update button in versions 7 & 8 automatically updates the purchase ledger from your processed orders.

4 Click on the Deliver button to update your product record details.

3 Enter the part quantity received in the This Delivery column.

New in Sage Line 50 v8, use the GRN button from the Purchase Order Processing toolbar to quickly produce Goods Received Notes.

5 Click Yes to confirm updating of order.

6 Click Close to finish & note status is PART.

Printing Batched Purchase Orders

Always make sure you have the correct stationery in the printer as the layout and content of the Purchase Order depends upon the stationery layout file selected.

Rather than print your Purchase Orders straight away you may have chosen to save them until later. This is useful if you only have one printer and need to change the stationery. When you are ready you can then print the orders out in batches.

As with all the printing facilities in Sage Line 50, you can send the Purchase Order direct to the printer, save it as a file or preview it on the screen first. To preview on order and then print it do the following:

1 From the Purchase Order Processing window, select the order for printing.

2 Click Print.

To print a specific selection of Purchase Orders use the Search button.

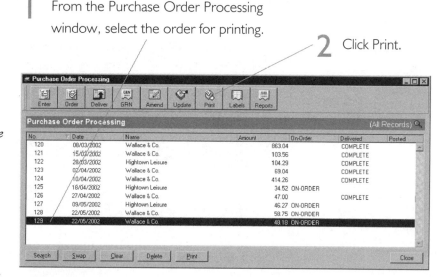

Your Purchase Orders can be reprinted as often as you wish.

3 Select correct layout.

4 Ensure Preview is checked.

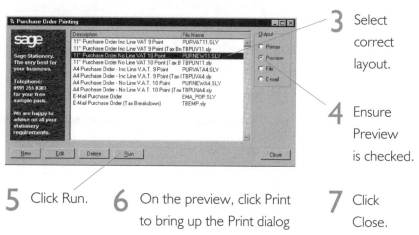

Save time by e-mailing your Purchase Orders directly to your Suppliers.

5 Click Run.

6 On the preview, click Print to bring up the Print dialog box, then click OK.

7 Click Close.

Purchase Order Reports

Standard reports have already been set up for you to display any outstanding Purchase Orders, or orders which have already been delivered or part delivered. These reports can be previewed on screen, sent to your printer or saved to a file for previewing or printing later.

To generate a report of Purchase Orders not yet delivered, do the following:

Use the Purchase Order Not Delivered or Part Delivered report to track and monitor your supplies.

To quickly view details of your Purchase Orders use the Purchase Orders List report.

Use the Outstanding Purchase Orders report regularly to keep track of which orders are still outstanding for delivery.

Use the Labels button from the Purchase Order Processing toolbar to quickly print Purchase Order Address and Stock labels.

1 From the Purchase Order Processing toolbar, click Reports.

2 Select required layout.

3 Check Output is set to Preview.

4 Click Run to view report.

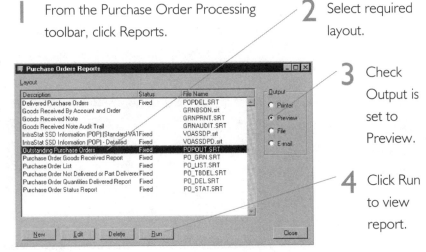

5 Enter Criteria, if any applies.

6 Click OK to generate the report.

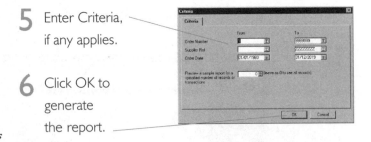

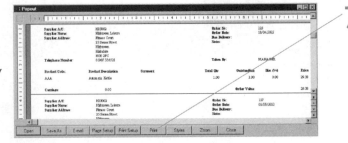

7 Click Print to send to printer, then OK & Close.

Financials

This Chapter shows you how to generate a variety of Financial reports so you can analyse your business transactions. This includes the Trial Balance, Profit & Loss, the Balance Sheet, the Budget and Prior Year reports. You will learn how to produce an automated VAT Return as well as a detailed Audit Trail, which lists every transaction recorded within the system.

Covers

Chapter Ten

The Financials Toolbar

From this toolbar you can generate all the financial reports you need to not only keep track of how your business is doing financially but also trace back and find out when certain transactions took place. The Audit Trail is particularly useful as it is a complete record of your transaction activities, whilst the VAT function gives you all the features you need to produce accurate VAT Returns.

 To Produce the Audit Trail.

 Run the Trial Balance Report.

 To Produce the Profit and Loss Report.

 To Produce the Balance Sheet Report.

 Run the Quick Ratio Report.

 To Produce the Budget Report.

 Run the Prior Year Report.

 To Produce a VAT Return.

 To Run Financial Reports.

The Audit Trail

Deleted transactions always appear in red.

Transaction codes used in the Audit Trail are explained on Page 49.

The Audit Trail records details about transactions entered into the system and is a very useful source of information for checking and cross reference purposes. It may also be referred to when auditing your accounts.

Sage Line 50 gives you a range of Audit Trail formats providing brief, summary or fully detailed reports which can be previewed, printed directly or saved as a file for use later. A report of deleted transactions can also be printed. Use the Audit Trail regularly to ensure your transactions are being recorded accurately. To view the Audit Trail:

1 From the Sage Line 50 toolbar, click Financials to bring up the Financials window displaying the Audit Trail.

Sage Line 50 is capable of storing approximately 2,000,000,000 transactions in the Audit Trail (provided your computer has sufficient memory and disk space), so there may be no need to clear it.

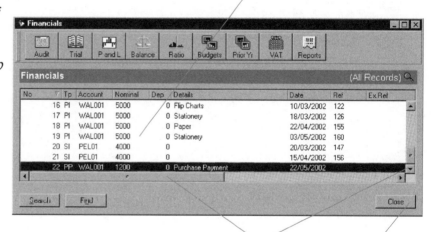

When you clear transactions from the Audit Trail, Sage Line 50 brings them forward as opening balances in your financial reports.

2 Use both horizontal and vertical arrow buttons and scroll bars to examine all transaction details.

3 When you have finished examining the Audit Trail, click Close.

To print the Audit Trail report

The Criteria box options vary according to the type of Audit Trail report selected.

1 From the Financials toolbar click Audit.

2 Select Audit Trail Type required, i.e. Brief.

3 Check Output is set to Preview.

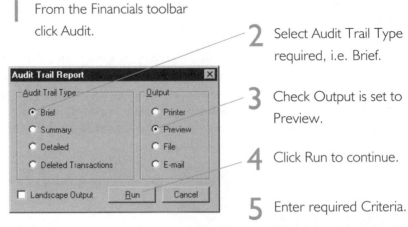

4 Click Run to continue.

All reports other than Brief will print in Landscape by default.

5 Enter required Criteria.

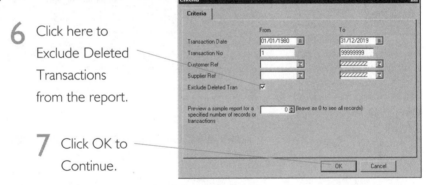

6 Click here to Exclude Deleted Transactions from the report.

You can choose to exclude deleted transactions from your reports and instead, print them as a separate report later.

7 Click OK to Continue.

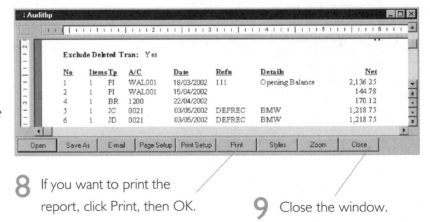

Print your Audit Trail reports at least every month for reference purposes.

8 If you want to print the report, click Print, then OK.

9 Close the window.

The Trial Balance

You can run this report for any month. It proves a valuable source for management information.

This report displays a simple listing of current balances in all your nominal ledger accounts. It shows total values for both the debit and credit entries for all the nominal codes containing a balance value.

Because Sage Line 50 controls the double-entry accounting for you, the debit and credit columns will always balance. To produce the Trial Balance report do the following:

 From the Financials toolbar click Trial. This brings up the Criteria box.

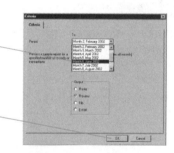

Use the Zoom feature to help you preview the report more accurately before printing.

2 Ensure Preview is selected.

3 Click here and select period required. Scroll down if necessary.

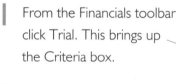

4 Click OK to generate the Trial Balance.

When you open the Financials window, the display automatically jumps down to the bottom of the list so the most recently entered transactions are displayed.

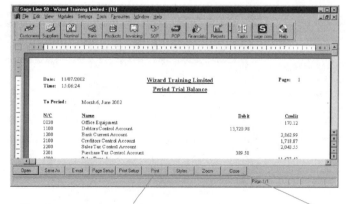

5 To print, click Print, then OK.

6 Click Close.

Profit and Loss Report

This important financial report details whether your business is trading at a profit over a particular period of time. The report can be produced for the current month or a range of consecutive months within your current financial year.

The balances of each of your income and expenditure nominal ledger accounts appear on the standard Profit and Loss report. These categories, i.e. Sales, Purchases, Direct Expenses and Overheads are grouped together and display a sub-total. The Gross Profit/(Loss) and Net Profit/(Loss) amount is also shown.

Balances are posted before the start of the financial year and so will appear as a prior year adjustment on the balance sheet, not on the Profit and Loss Report.

1 From the Financials window click P and L to bring up the Criteria box.

Unless you have set up your own layout, ensure you choose the Default Layout of Accounts in Step 3, otherwise you will not generate the correct report.

2 Enter the From and To Period required.

3 Select Default Layout of Accounts (1).

4 Ensure Preview is selected.

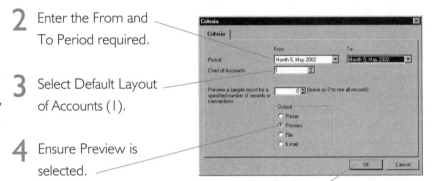

5 Click OK to generate P & L report.

You can set up your own Profit & Loss report layouts using the Chart of Accounts option from the Nominal Ledger toolbar.

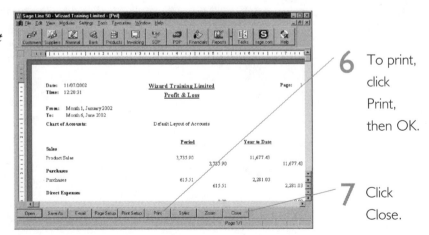

6 To print, click Print, then OK.

7 Click Close.

The Balance Sheet

Use the Balance Sheet regularly to give a summary of your current financial position.

The Balance Sheet details the financial position of a business at a particular moment in time by outlining its assets (what the business owns) and its liabilities (what the business owes). There are two main types of assets, fixed and current. Fixed assets are long-term and have material substance and include, for example, premises, equipment and vehicles, whilst current assets are continually changing and include stock, debtors, cash accounts etc.

The Balance Sheet shows the fixed and current assets, as well as the liabilities. By adding together the assets and subtracting the liabilities, the Balance Sheet shows the Capital, or net assets.

The difference between assets and liabilities is referred to as the company's net assets (or net worth).

1 Click Balance from the Financials toolbar to display the Criteria box.

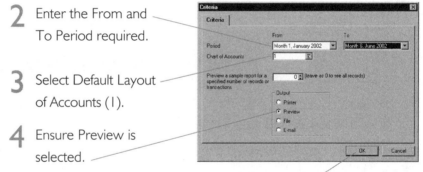

2 Enter the From and To Period required.

3 Select Default Layout of Accounts (1).

Liabilities consist of both current and long-term. Current liabilities are amounts owing at the balance sheet date and due for repayment within 12 months or less, e.g. trade creditors. Long-term liabilities are amounts due for repayment in more than 12 months, e.g. bank loan.

4 Ensure Preview is selected.

5 Click OK to generate Balance Sheet.

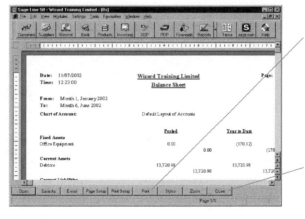

6 To print the Balance Sheet, click Print, then OK.

7 Click Close.

Quick Ratio Report

Use the Quick Ratio Report to see the immediate financial position of your company. This is useful when you are considering future investments etc.

Using the data available within the system, the Quick Ratio Report allows you to see the current liquidity position of the business. This type of information is necessary for making financial decisions about future investments or developments and will be required by a number of different parties, for example, management, bank managers, shareholders etc.

These Ratio Reports highlight both the strengths and the weaknesses in the financial position of your business. Credit and debit balances are compared to show the net balance using previously set up nominal account codes. You can edit the report to include other nominal accounts you wish to compare.

To view or edit the quick ratio report

By editing the Quick Ratio Report you can include different nominal accounts for comparison purposes.

1 From the Financials window, click Ratio.

2 To edit the nominal accounts, use Finder button to select Nominal Code required.

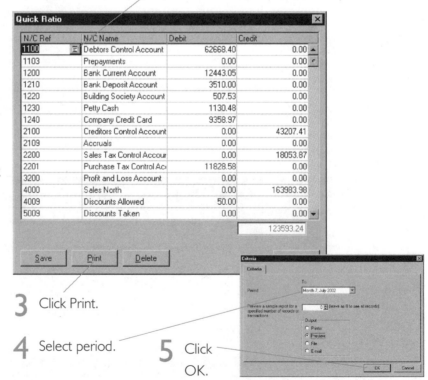

N/C Ref	N/C Name	Debit	Credit
1100	Debtors Control Account	62668.40	0.00
1103	Prepayments	0.00	0.00
1200	Bank Current Account	12443.05	0.00
1210	Bank Deposit Account	3510.00	0.00
1220	Building Society Account	507.53	0.00
1230	Petty Cash	1130.48	0.00
1240	Company Credit Card	9358.97	0.00
2100	Creditors Control Account	0.00	43207.41
2109	Accruals	0.00	0.00
2200	Sales Tax Control Accour	0.00	18053.87
2201	Purchase Tax Control Aci	11828.58	0.00
3200	Profit and Loss Account	0.00	0.00
4000	Sales North	0.00	163983.98
4009	Discounts Allowed	50.00	0.00
5009	Discounts Taken	0.00	0.00

123593.24

Save   Print   Delete

Use the F4 key to speedily open or close a drop-down list box as required.

Click the Save button to store a Quick Ratio report for future reference.

3 Click Print.

4 Select period.

5 Click OK.

The Budget Report

You can amend your nominal account Budget values at any time by using the Global Changes feature from the Tools menu.

The Budget Report displays the current values in your purchases, sales, direct expenses and overhead account codes for the months you select and the year-to-date. Use this report to see how your business actually traded compared with the monthly budget you set against the nominal ledger accounts for the chosen months and the year to date.

| Click Budgets from the Financials toolbar.

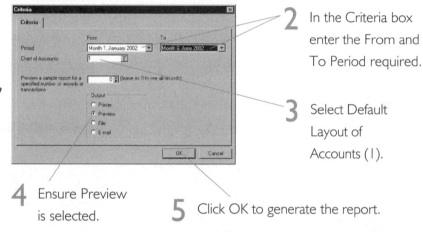

2 In the Criteria box enter the From and To Period required.

3 Select Default Layout of Accounts (1).

When you run a year end, Sage Line 50 offers you the option to move the actual monthly values for the year just ended to the budgets for the coming year. This sets the budget values to be what really happened in each month of the year just ended. You can also add a percentage increase to your budget values to reflect any anticipated rise in sales, purchases, costs, etc. for the coming year.

4 Ensure Preview is selected.

5 Click OK to generate the report.

It is preferable to send an e-mailed report as a html attachment.

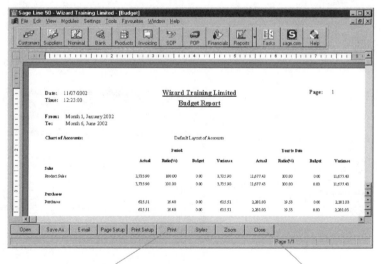

6 To print, click Print, then OK.

7 Click Close.

The Prior Year Report

Use the Prior Year report to compare your current trading results against how you did for the same period last year.

The Prior Year report compares the current values in your purchases, sales, direct expenses and overhead accounts codes using the formats as set up for you in your chart of accounts. Trading activities are detailed for both the current month and the year-to-date, or alternatively for any period you specify.

This report compares how your business is trading for the specified period against the same period in the previous year. Year-to-date totals and ratios are also included. To produce a Prior Year report, from the Financials window do the following:

You can create your own report layouts for different Chart of Accounts.

1 Click Prior Yr to bring up the Criteria box.

2 Select Period required here.

3 Select Default Layout of Accounts (1).

To make a Prior Year Adjustment for your business refer to the Sage Line 50 Help Library Topics and search for Prior Year.

4 Check Output is set to Preview.

5 Click OK to continue.

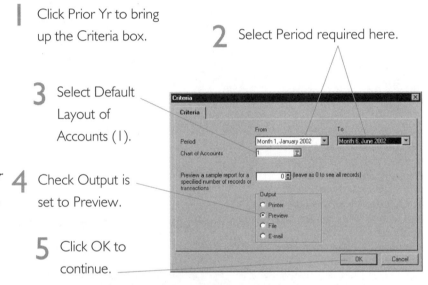

If you wish to create a new Chart of Accounts layout simply refer to Page 55.

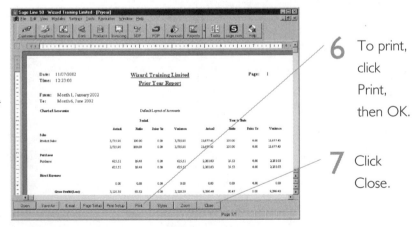

6 To print, click Print, then OK.

7 Click Close.

The VAT Return

Use the Wizard button to guide you through the VAT Return process.

For businesses that need to submit VAT Return forms to HM Customs & Excise, Sage Line 50 version 8 provides all the features to enable you to do this quickly and accurately, calculating both input and output tax for you from the information you have entered over the period. This is a prime reason for keeping accurate accounts.

Input tax is the VAT you are charged on your business purchases and expenses. Output tax is the VAT your business charges on its taxable supplies or services. Because Value Added Tax is a tax charged to the final consumer, a business needs to calculate what input tax can be reclaimed and how much output tax needs paying to Customs & Excise. This is the purpose of the VAT Return.

Before reconciling your VAT transactions, you should back up your data files. Reconciling your transactions sets a flag against each transaction so it is automatically excluded from subsequent VAT Returns.

You have the facility to set up 100 tax codes, but on installation Sage Line 50 sets the standard UK and EC VAT rates for you, so you will probably not have to change anything. The default is set to the standard rate T1, presently at 17.5%, whilst others you may need are T0 (zero-rated) and T9 (transactions not involving VAT).

Within the nominal ledger are three accounts, namely the Sales Tax Control account (2200), Purchase Tax Control account (2201) and VAT liability account (2202). An accumulated total appears in the Sales account for the output tax charged to your customers whilst another accumulated total appears in the Purchase account for the input tax charged to your business.

When your VAT Return is due, enter the correct date range into the system and the program will calculate the difference between the input and output tax and will inform you of the net VAT due to either the Customs & Excise or yourselves.

The Audit Trail VAT column shows whether a transaction is reconciled or not:

- *R = reconciled;*
- *N = unreconciled;*
- *a hyphen (-) or a dash (–) = a non-VAT transaction.*

After reconciling your VAT Return, VAT on the Sales and Purchases Control accounts for this VAT period need transferring to the VAT Liability nominal account. When a bank payment to the Customs & Excise is made or received, the VAT Liability account is cleared, leaving a zero balance.

...cont'd

To produce your VAT Return

Ensure all transactions have been reconciled and the Audit Trail checked before running your VAT Return.

1 From the Financials window click VAT to bring up the VAT Return window displaying zero totals.

2 Enter the inclusive VAT period dates here.

Use the Wizard button to guide you through the VAT Return process.

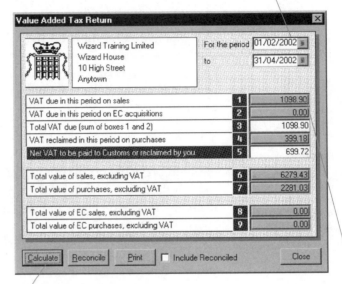

Use the Calculate button to automatically calculate the totals for your VAT Return.

3 Click Calculate to calculate totals for this return. You will be informed if any unreconciled transactions have been found.

4 Click on a VAT total for a breakdown.

Three reports are available for printing: Detailed, Summary and the VAT Return. The Detailed and Summary reports give a breakdown of all the totals from each box on the VAT Return.

5 Double-click on a Tax Code for a transaction breakdown.

6 Close each window to return to VAT Return.

7 Click Print, Run and OK to print the return.

Check that the balance of your VAT Return agrees with the balance of your VAT Control Accounts.

The VAT Transfer Wizard

Use the VAT Transfer Wizard to guide you through the transfer of your VAT liability once you have successfully reconciled and printed your VAT return.

1 From the Line 50 menu, click Modules, select Wizards, then click VAT Transfer Wizard.

2 Click Yes to confirm you wish to continue.

Use the VAT Transfer Wizard to transfer money from the Sales and Purchase Tax Control accounts to the VAT Liability account.

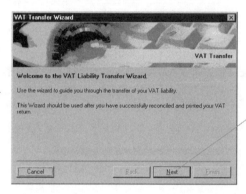

3 Click Next to proceed with the Wizard.

Note that Sage Line 50 already has the following tax rates set up:

T0 = zero rated transactions.

T1 = standard rate.

T2 = exempt transactions.

T4 = sales to customers in EC.

T7 = zero rated purchases from suppliers in EC.

T8 = standard rated purchases from suppliers in EC.

T9 = transactions not involving VAT.

4 Work your way through each screen entering details where required and clicking Next until you reach the Confirm Posting Details window.

5 Click Finish to confirm details or Cancel to discard.

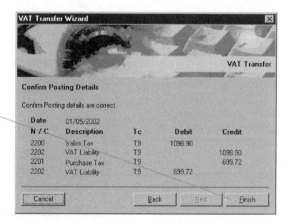

Financial Reports

Sage Line 50 version 8 offers a wide range of Financial Reports that provide management information to enable effective decision making, planning and forecasting.

A considerable number of reports are set up at installation time, but many can be customised if required for your business by changing the appearance of the layout, the font type or by adding/removing certain text. Refer to Chapter Twelve for more details. To generate a report:

With Sage Line 50 versions 7 & 8 you can calculate profit and loss for the current month or for any range of consecutive months within your current financial year.

1 From the Financials toolbar click Reports.

2 Select the report layout required.

3 Check Output is set to Preview.

4 Click Run to view the report.

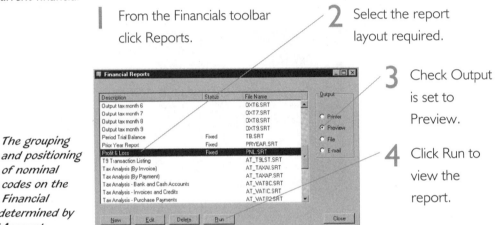

The grouping and positioning of nominal codes on the Financial Reports are determined by the Chart of Account.

5 Enter appropriate Criteria here.

6 Click OK to generate the report.

Information used for creating Financial Reports is taken from the actuals column in the Nominal Ledger Record.

7 Click Print to send to printer, then OK and Close.

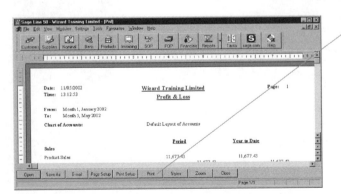

Fixed Assets

This Chapter explains how to work with Fixed Asset Records and how to view the value of your assets by running Fixed Asset Reports. It also details the three accepted methods of depreciation offered by Sage Line 50, enabling you to decide which is the most appropriate method to use for your business.

Covers

Chapter Eleven

The Fixed Assets Toolbar

This toolbar features options for creating Fixed Asset Records and setting up the method of depreciation, performing valuation of Fixed Assets and the generation of your Fixed Asset reports.

To Create a Fixed Asset Record.

To Report on Asset Valuation.

To Dispose a Fixed Asset.

To Run Fixed Asset Reports.

Note:

In Sage Line 50 version 8 there is no Fixed Assets button on the Toolbar. Instead, do the following to bring up the Fixed Assets window:

1   On the Sage Line 50 menu bar, click Modules.

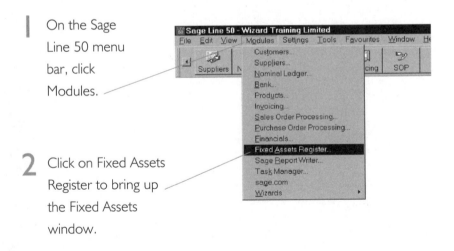

2   Click on Fixed Assets Register to bring up the Fixed Assets window.

Recording your Fixed Assets

Fixed Assets are items such as office equipment, buildings, machinery, etc. owned by the business. Their depreciation is an expense and can be offset against profits.

However, before recording Fixed Asset information, it is important that the correct method and rate of depreciation be decided upon and applied consistently. Different classes of Fixed Assets are often depreciated at different rates, for example, office furniture may be depreciated at a different rate to motor vehicles.

Sage Line 50 offers the choice of three depreciation methods: Straight Line, Reducing Balance and Write Off. For the Straight Line method, the asset is depreciated by a fixed percentage (calculated from the original Cost Price of the asset) every month until the asset is reduced to zero. For the Reducing Balance method, the asset is depreciated again monthly by a fixed percentage, but this time the percentage is applied to the new book value of the asset.

The last method, Write Off depreciation, makes one last posting to depreciate the remaining value of the asset.

When ready to enter your fixed assets for the first time you will notice that the Fixed Assets window is empty. As soon as Fixed Asset Records are entered, they will be displayed one record per line. To bring up the Fixed Assets window:

| From Modules, click Fixed Assets Register.

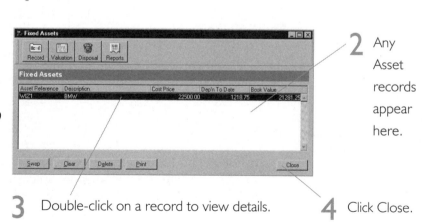

2 Any Asset records appear here.

3 Double-click on a record to view details.

4 Click Close.

Adding Fixed Asset Records.

The first time you use the Assets option, the Fixed Assets window will be empty. To add a Fixed Asset record, have all the necessary information to hand, then do the following:

You cannot save a new record unless the nominal ledger posting details have been entered.

1 From the Fixed Assets toolbar click Record.

2 Enter a unique code to easily identify asset, e.g., WIZ2 (no spaces allowed).

3 Type a Description here.

Use the Tab key to move to the next data entry box.

4 Enter a Serial Number for extra information.

Fixed Asset Record
Details	Posting
Asset Reference: WIZ2   New Asset
Description: ROVER
Serial Number: WIZ2
Location/Emp'ee:
Date Purchased: 11/06/2002   Supplier A/C: GAR001
Asset Category: 1
Save   Delete   Discard   <   >   Close

To delete an Asset, simply highlight it in the Fixed Assets window, then click on the Delete button.

5 Enter Location if relevant.

6 Enter Date Purchased.

7 If the asset was bought from one of your current Suppliers, select A/C here.

8 For reporting purposes you can categorise your fixed assets. Select Asset Category from drop down list here.

Use the Clear button to quickly deselect all selected records.

Although you have now entered all the relevant details for this asset, before you can save this new record you still need to enter the appropriate nominal ledger posting details. This is explained on the next two pages.

Fixed Asset Depreciation

The Fixed Asset option does not post depreciation for you, only records the asset and current value. Use Month End option to automatically make monthly depreciation postings.

The Posting Tab is used for entering the necessary nominal ledger posting details. Then, when you run the Month End/Year End depreciation posting routines, asset depreciation will be added to the appropriate account code as an expense to your business and will be shown on the balance sheet and profit and loss report.

There are four depreciation accounts already set up in the balance sheet of the nominal ledger by Sage Line 50. Every time an asset is depreciated, the amount of depreciation is posted as a credit posting. Codes include 0021 (Plant/Machinery Depreciation), 0031 (Office Equipment Depreciation), 0041 (Furniture/Fixture Depreciation) and 0051 (Motor Vehicles Depreciation).

Once you have saved a record, the depreciation method can only ever be changed to Write Off.

Similarly, four depreciation accounts are already set up for you in the profit & loss section of the nominal ledger. Every time an asset is depreciated, the value of that depreciation is added to the account code as an expense to the company (debit posting). Codes include 8001 (Plant/Machinery Depreciation), 8002 (Furniture/Fitting Depreciation), 8003 (Vehicle Depreciation) and 8004 (Office Equipment Depreciation).

Once a depreciation posting has been made by the Month End/Year End routines for this asset, the Cost Price or Book Value cannot be changed.

You need to enter the annual rate of depreciation. For the Straight Line method, the value entered will be divided by twelve to calculate the monthly depreciation. For example, to depreciate an asset completely over five years using the straight line method, the Dep'n Rate would be 20%, depreciating at 1.666% monthly until after five years the book value is zero. So, for an item costing £15,000, a depreciation value of £250 would be posted for 60 months.

To record a Fixed Asset Disposal simply click on the Disposal button on the Fixed Assets toolbar and follow the step-by-step Wizard prompt screens.

Where Book Value details are required, then enter the current book value. If the asset is brand new, this should be the same as the Cost Price. If an asset has already been depreciated, then enter the cost price minus depreciation. If the reducing balance method was selected, the Book Value will be used to calculate the depreciation amount. Sage Line 50 will automatically reduce this value by the depreciation amount during the month end procedure.

You must have all the details of the asset to be disposed to hand before running the Fixed Asset Disposal Wizard.

Depreciation and Valuation

Setting up a Fixed Asset depreciation posting

From the Fixed Assets window, click the Valuation button to quickly check the total cost, total current book value and the total amount of depreciation that has taken place so far on all of your asset records.

1 After entering the Fixed Asset Record details (page 136) select the Posting tab.

2 Select Department where appropriate.

3 Enter nominal ledger balance sheet account code.

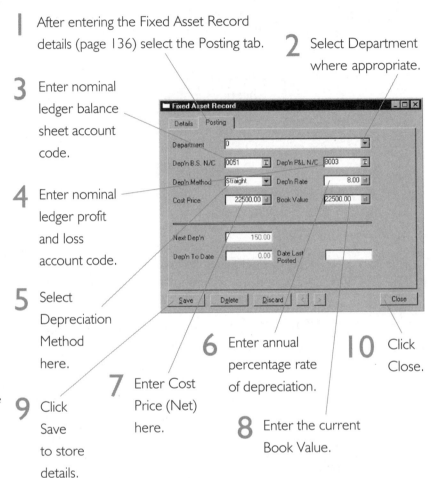

To run a Fixed Asset report, click Reports from the Fixed Assets toolbar and select one of the ready set up reports included with Sage Line 50.

4 Enter nominal ledger profit and loss account code.

5 Select Depreciation Method here.

6 Enter annual percentage rate of depreciation.

7 Enter Cost Price (Net) here.

8 Enter the current Book Value.

10 Click Close.

With Sage Line 50 versions 7 & 8 you can also save non-depreciating assets as well as depreciation assets.

9 Click Save to store details.

Valuation of Fixed Assets

To see details about the current value of your assets including total cost, previous total depreciation and total current book value do the following:

Refer to Sage Help for easy instructions plus an example on recording Higher Purchase Agreements, including Part Exchange.

1 From the Fixed Assets window click Valuation to bring up the Asset Valuation window.

2 When finished, click Close.

The Report Designer

This chapter shows you how to create a new report and also how to edit an existing report to meet your own requirements. Report Designer is very powerful and provides options for grouping and sorting information, adding calculations such as totals, setting up criteria and filters to search for information as well as designing the layout and format of the report.

Covers

Chapter Twelve

Introducing the Report Designer

For more details about the Report Designer, click Reports from the Sage Line 50 toolbar and press F1.

When you first install Sage Line 50, you can immediately generate and print all of the reports and stationery to suit most business needs. If you use stationery supplied by Sage, the data should fit in the pre-printed stationery forms without adjustment.

There will be occasions though when you need a new report not already supplied, or you need to modify an existing one to suit your specific needs. The Report Designer lets you do all of this to meet any specific requirements that you have.

You may need to click on the right scroll button on the Sage Line 50 toolbar a few times to bring the Report button into view, depending on the screen area setting for your computer.

The Report Designer, although an integral part of Sage Line 50, is actually a complete windows application on its own. The Designer has its own Title Bar, Menu Bar, and Desktop area on which you can open multiple document windows. Each document window can hold an entirely separate layout file, which means you can work on several layouts at once, if you wish. To run Report Designer:

1 Select the Report button from the Sage Line 50 toolbar.

2 The Report Designer window appears.

Use Report Designer to design new (or modify existing) reports to fit into any new pre-printed stationery forms your business may adopt.

3 Click here on each folder to see a list of existing layouts.

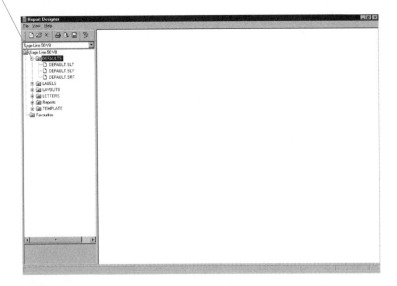

Use the Report Designer to create your own reports, stationery layouts, letters and labels.

Creating a New Report

When the Wizard is finished the Report Designer appears with the new report/layout open ready for you to work on or preview.

When your new report is complete, you can either save, preview, or print it.

You can also double-click the required variable to copy it to the Report Variables view.

For information about the variables, click the Variable Info button. You can then print out the variable list for reference.

Use the Favourites option in Sage Line 50 Version 7 or 8 to access frequently used reports.

The following example shows you how to create a Customer Balance and Credit List for a single customer or a range of customers using the Report Wizard. The report contains the Customer's account reference, company name and account balance, together with their credit limit. The report is sorted to show the customer with the lowest balance first. The report also displays a balance total.

1 From the Sage Line 50 toolbar select Reports.

2 Click File and New from the Report Designer menu, then click Next.

3 Select Customer option.

4 Enter report Title here.

5 Click Next to continue.

6 Select variable required from this list.

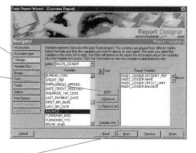

7 Click Add button to copy to Report Variables view.

8 Repeat Step 7 for all required variables.

9 Click Next and Next again.

10 Grouping is not required, so just click Next again.

11 Select SALES_ LEDGER.BALANCE.

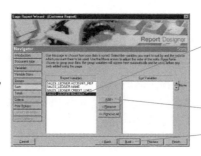

12 Click the Add button.

13 Click Next.

14 Select SALES_LEDGER.CREDIT_LIMIT.

Only numeric variables will be listed to total on when designing your report.

15 This total is not required, so click Remove to remove it from the list.

16 Click Next.

Criteria Status can be set to Disabled, Enabled or Preset. This controls the Criteria screen that appears prior to running the report.

17 Set Status to Enabled for Customer Ref and Tran Date.

18 Click Next.

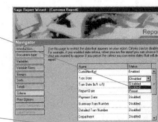

Choose Preset for the Criteria Status to enter dates that will always be used for the report.

19 Make any necessary changes to the printing options, i.e., Paper size or report Orientation.

20 Click Finish to generate the report layout.

Should you ever need to remove all the Total Variables simply click the << Remove All button.

The Report Designer now generates the appropriate report layout for you. You will be able to see how the layout is divided into sections, i.e., Page Header, Details, Page Footer, etc.

If the layout is not as required, you can modify the report later. First you need to check that it provides the information you require by running a report preview.

Previewing your Report

Maximise your report layout window to view all the variables.

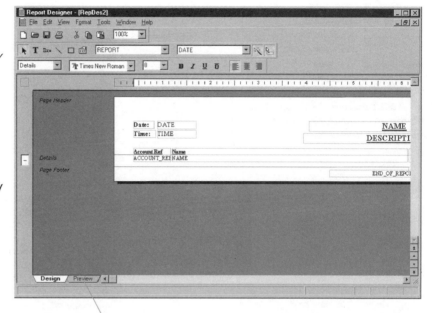

Your report will appear in your Customers Reports window after saving.

I Click Preview to run your new report.

2 The Criteria box appears.

To speed up report design you can cut and paste groups of variables between two similar reports.

3 Enter Criteria details.

4 Click OK to run the report.

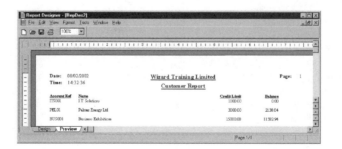

Be careful not to overwrite any existing reports. They may be useful to you later.

6 To close, click on File and Exit.

5 To save, select Save As from File menu, enter a filename and click OK.

Modifying an Existing Report

To remove your company's name and address from all your layout files, select Company Preferences from the Settings menu on the Sage Line 50 toolbar. Click on the Parameters tab and deselect the Print Address on Stationery check box, then click OK.

The Report Designer lets you modify existing report layout files and default reports supplied with the program. These will, however, need saving under a new filename.

As an example, you can modify the report just created and saved to include only customers with a balance greater than £1000. This is called a filter, which is embedded in the report layout. To make these changes it is easier to start from the Sage Line 50 Customers option:

1 From the Customer toolbar click on the Reports option.

2 Select your report from the list and click Edit.

3 Click Format, Filter.

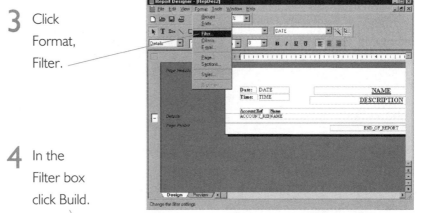

You can edit some Fixed Reports and save them to a new filename. The original report remains unchanged and your new report is added to the list.

4 In the Filter box click Build.

If you make a mistake designing the report, select immediately the Edit Undo option from the Edit menu.

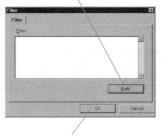

7 Click OK, Preview & Save.

5 Select Sales_Ledger.Credit_Limit and click Add.

6 Click > and type 1000 here, then OK.

Opening Balances

This chapter explains how to enter opening balances for your customer, supplier, nominal and bank accounts as well as your products.

Covers

Chapter Thirteen

Introduction

Print off a copy of the Opening Balances checklist from the F1 Help system to guide you.

It is important to set up opening balances correctly and in the right order. All accounts remain at zero until you enter opening balances for your Customers, Suppliers, Nominal, Bank and Products.

Where opening balances are carried forward, accurate figures need entering to indicate the true financial position of the business, for example, its Debtors, Creditors, Nominal Ledger Trial Balance, as well as its Stock.

Posted Opening Balances for your customers and suppliers are displayed in the trial balance report, which needs clearing before entering Opening Balances for the nominal ledger account, bank account and products.

Standard VAT and VAT Cash Accounting

Standard VAT calculates the VAT return on the invoices/credits you have raised for your customers or received from your suppliers, and any bank/cash payments or receipts or journal entries with vatable tax codes.

Customer opening balances can be entered as lump sum balances. It is recommended, however, that each outstanding invoice and credit note be entered separately for cross referencing. Recording separate transactions will also provide accurate aged debtors analysis.

The second method, the VAT Cash Accounting scheme, is where the VAT return is calculated on the invoices/credits which you have received payment for from your customers or you have paid to your suppliers. Included too are any bank/cash payments or receipts or journal entries with vatable tax codes.

Note that these are the Nominal Codes used in the Trial Balance:

1100 = Debtors Control Account.

2100 = Creditors Control Account.

9998 = Suspense Account.

With VAT Cash Accounting each invoice and credit note must be entered for your customers individually, with the correct tax code.

The same Standard VAT and VAT Cash Accounting conditions apply for entering opening balances for suppliers. Again, it is recommended for Standard VAT that separate transactions be recorded for outstanding invoices and credit notes to match up with payments later instead of grouping them all together in one opening balance. Separate transactions will again provide accurate aged creditors information.

Opening Balances – Standard VAT

Follow the same procedures as for Customers when entering opening balances for your Suppliers.

When entering a total for outstanding invoices/credit notes, O/BAL is a useful reference.

By recording the original invoice/credit note date, you will have accurate details of overdue debtors.

Use Next and Back buttons to move between customers.

With the Standard VAT accounting method opening balances can be entered as a lump sum or individual transactions. You set up your customer balances using the Customer Record, accessed by using the Customers button on the Sage Line 50 toolbar.

Where customer information exists already, you can refer to the Aged Debtors Analysis and Detailed Customer Activity reports for cross referencing purposes and for checking that opening balances are recorded accurately. The Aged Creditors and Detailed Supplier Activity reports are also available for your suppliers.

To enter customer Opening Balance details

1 From the Customers window click on the required record, then click Record on the toolbar.

2 Click here to set up Opening Balance.

An Opening Balance can be entered as one total amount if a detailed breakdown is not required.

3 Enter invoice/credit note number.

4 Enter original transaction date or last date of previous financial year.

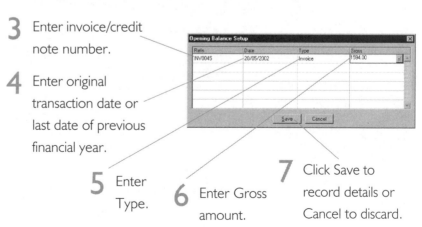

5 Enter Type.

6 Enter Gross amount.

7 Click Save to record details or Cancel to discard.

T9 is set as the default non-vatable tax code.

Opening Balances – VAT Cash Accounting

To enter Opening Balances for your suppliers, click on the Suppliers button, then follow the steps you would with Customers.

Using this particular scheme each customer invoice and credit note needs entering individually with the correct tax code because VAT is only considered when payment is being made. The opening balances can be entered via the Batch Invoices or Credits screens.

To enter customer Opening Balance details

I From the Customers window click on the required record, then click Record on the toolbar.

Use Audit Trail from Financials to identify reference numbers.

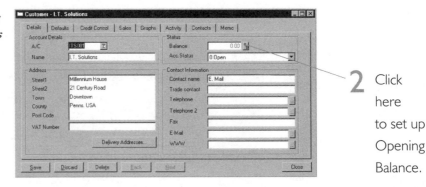

2 Click here to set up Opening Balance.

Enter original date of invoice or credit note for accurate aged debtors analysis or last date of previous financial year.

3 Enter invoice/credit note number.

4 Enter original transaction date or last date of previous financial year.

The default tax code and VAT appear automatically, but can be changed if necessary.

5 Enter Type.

6 Enter Net amount. If you want to enter a single opening balance for this customer, enter total net amount of all invoices here.

7 Tax Code and VAT are entered for you. Change if necessary then click Save to record details or Cancel to discard.

Clearing Opening Balances From Trial Balance

Always print a copy of your Trial Balance report BEFORE clearing the opening balances.

When opening balances for your customers and suppliers are saved, they are posted to the trial balance. These entries need clearing or they will be duplicated when posting opening balances for your nominal ledger accounts. This will produce an incorrect balance sheet.

Before you start, make a note from your trial balance of the values of your Debtors and Creditors Control Accounts, your Sales Tax and Purchase Tax Control Accounts and your Suspense Account and whether each one is a debit or a credit, for example:

If you are using VAT Cash Accounting, balances need clearing in your Sales and Purchase Tax Control Accounts.

Trial Balance

Name	TC	Debit	Credit
Debtors Control Account	T9	30,687.19	
Creditors Control Account	T9		21,189.78
Suspense	T9		9,497.41
BALANCE		30,687.19	30,687.19

When entering journal entries into the transaction table, use opposite values from the trial balance, i.e., Debit (+) and Credit (-).

Once the relevant details have been noted, a Journal Entry from the Nominal Ledger needs to be made to clear the balances. Using the details from the above example, the entry would be as follows:

Journal Entry

Name	TC	Debit	Credit
Debtors Control Account	T9		30,687.19
Creditors Control Account	T9	21,189.78	
Suspense	T9	9,497.41	
BALANCE		30,687.19	30,687.19

The journal entry can only be saved when the value in the Balance box is zero.

Once you have noted what entries you need to make, you can add them to the Journal. When you process these entries, the opening balances in the Trial Balance will be cleared. To make the entries do the following:

Always bear in mind that for a journal entry, VAT is neither calculated for you nor posted to the VAT control account.

1 From the Sage Line 50 toolbar click Nominal.

2 Click on Journals from the Nominal Ledger window to bring up the Journals window.

3 The Ref. entry is optional. Type a reference if desired.

4 Check for correct Date.

Use the Finder button to quickly locate the correct codes.

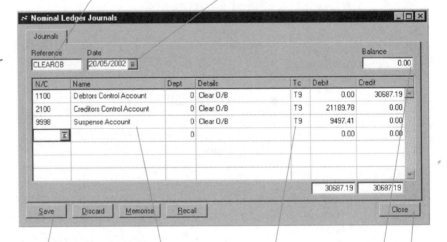

N/C	Name	Dept	Details	Tc	Debit	Credit
1100	Debtors Control Account	0	Clear O/B	T9	0.00	30687.19
2100	Creditors Control Account	0	Clear O/B	T9	21189.78	0.00
9998	Suspense Account	0	Clear O/B	T9	9497.41	0.00
		0			0.00	0.00
					30687.19	30687.19

Reference: CLEAROB Date: 20/05/2002 Balance: 0.00

Save Discard Memorise Recall Close

If you make a mistake just click on the Discard button and start again.

5 Enter details for both the credit and debits.

6 Note, the default Tax code of T9 is entered for you by Sage Line 50.

7 Check total Debit and Credit are equal and a zero balance is displayed in the Balance box.

8 Click Save to process your journal or Discard to cancel.

9 Click Close to return to Nominal Ledger window.

Entering Balances Part Way Through the Year

Sage Line 50 needs Opening Balances in order to produce accurate financial statements. Because all accounts in all the ledgers have a zero balance when the program is first installed, it is important that the Opening Balances are entered as soon as possible. Without them your financial statements will not be accurate.

When you use Sage Line 50 for the first time and you set up Product records, this is also a good time to have a stock take so that you know the details you are entering are accurate. Sage Line 50 can only produce accurate reports if the information you enter is correct. This is also a good time to check that Customer and Supplier details are still up to date.

It is, however, quite possible to start using Sage Line 50 at any time through your financial year, and then enter the Opening Balances as they become available. For instance, if you have been in business for some time you will already have stock, products, customers and suppliers. You will have a transaction history. When you first start to use Sage Line 50 you will set up Records for your Customers, Suppliers, Products etc. This is when you can start to enter some Opening Balances.

If you do start to use Sage Line 50 part way through your financial year, you should contact your accountant as soon as possible for a detailed list showing all your outstanding Debtors and Creditors. You can then use this as the Opening Balances for your Customers and Suppliers.

If you do not enter a Cost Price in the Opening Product Setup box, the product code is recorded as zero. This could affect your finance reports later.

You also need to ask for a Trial Balance from your accountant, which will give you the Opening Balances for each Nominal Ledger and Bank account.

You must at all times make sure that the information you enter is accurate. If you need to enter Opening Balances part way through your financial year, you will probably have a lot of Nominal Ledger opening balances to enter! It is important, therefore, that you enter these accurately otherwise your balance sheet will be incorrect.

You will also need to enter any year-to-date values from your Profit and Loss accounts. Your accountant should be able to provide you with this.

Nominal Ledger and Bank Account

When entering opening balances for your Nominal Ledger or Bank account, double-entry postings are applied by Sage Line 50. For example, if you post a debit opening balance of £100 to your Building Society account (1220 by default), Sage Line 50 automatically posts £100 as a credit to your Suspense Account (9998 by default).

After you have entered all your Nominal Ledger and Bank account opening balances, the balance of the Suspense Account should be zero again. A new trial balance needs printing to check opening balances have been included for all your nominal accounts. If you still have a balance in your Suspense Account (i.e. it is not zero), an opening balance may have been omitted or a debit or credit misposted.

Nominal ledger opening balances

If you have money in the bank or building society, their statement shows you have a balance under the credit column. They owe you that money, you are the creditor. When this money is recorded in your accounts, such asset balances are recorded the opposite way round as debits. If you have money in your bank or building society, the balance must be entered as a debit.

1 From the Sage Line 50 toolbar, select Nominal.

2 Click on the required account.

3 Click on the Record button.

Enter an opening balance for each nominal account code that appears on your trial balance.

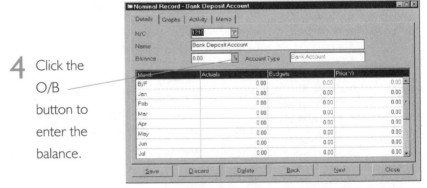

4 Click the O/B button to enter the balance.

5 Enter opening balance details here.

6 Click Save, then Close.

Bank Opening Balances

You can also set up a Bank account Opening Balance directly from the Bank Record. To do this follow these steps:

You can enter Bank account opening balances either through the Bank Record or through the Nominal Ledger Record, but not both.

1 From the Sage Line 50 toolbar, select Bank.

2 Click on the Bank Record you wish to set up an Opening Balance for and click on Record.

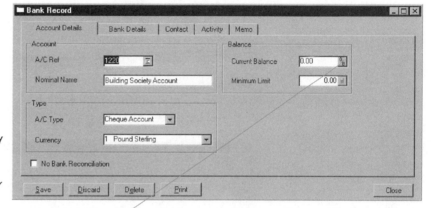

An asset should always have a debit entry, whilst a liability should always have a credit entry.

3 Click the O/B button to bring up the Opening Balance Setup box.

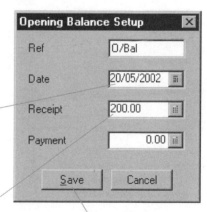

4 Enter Date if different from default date.

If you have money in your bank account, i.e., a debit, enter it as a Receipt. If you are overdrawn, i.e., a credit, enter it as a Payment.

5 Enter opening balance as a Receipt or Payment. If you have money in your bank, this will be a Receipt.

6 Click Save to record the Opening balance information.

Opening Balances for Products

If you have selected the Ignore Stock Levels check box, you cannot enter an opening balance for this product.

When you create a Product Record, you will probably enter an Opening Balance for that product if you already have some in stock. However, there will be times when you need to enter an Opening Balance at a later date to that when the Record was set up.

If you do the latter, when you save the Opening Balance for a product, Sage Line 50 posts an Adjustment In transaction, which appears on the product reports. The valuation report will show the opening stock quantity at the cost price entered. To set up a Product Opening Balance:

If you select more than one Product Record, use the Back and Next buttons to move through them in turn.

1 From the Sage Line 50 toolbar, click Products.

2 Select the Product or products requiring an opening balance.

3 Click Record.

4 Click O/B button on the In Stock box.

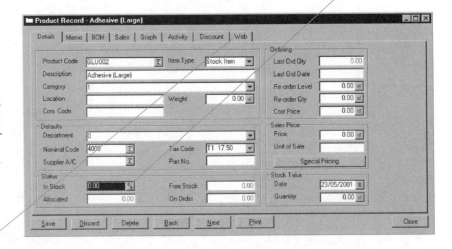

Do not forget to enter the Cost Price for the Product when you set up the Opening Balance.

To store a JPEG image of the item with the stock record select the Web tab and click on the Add button in the Image section.

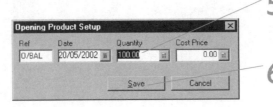

5 Enter Opening Balance details here.

6 Click Save to return to the Products Record, then Close.

Data Management

This chapter shows you important routines and procedures you need to use regularly for taking care of your data. Often data entered into the system is lost or corrupted by not following simple file maintenance. Backing up of data is essential to any business as problems often occur at the most inconvenient and crucial times.

Covers

Chapter Fourteen

Backing Up Data

It is advisable to run the data check option before you back up your data.

Regular data backup (at least once daily) is essential in case of system error, when valuable data can be corrupted and sometimes lost. If this happens, you can at least restore important data files, reports and/or layout templates from your most up-to-date backup. A backup routine is provided by Sage Line 50 to automatically backup to your computer's Floppy Drive A:, but this can be changed to save to any drive and/or directory you require.

Always keep your backups in a safe, secure place.

Backing up procedures vary from business to business; some use five disks for Monday to Friday and repeat their usage the following week. The important thing is to backup your data at least once a day! Sage Line 50 always prompts you to back up when you Exit the program, but to perform a backup at any other time, do the following:

Use the Options button in the Backup Data Files dialog to select what to backup – all your files, just your reports and/ or layout templates, or only your data files.

1 From the Sage Line 50 menu, click on File.

2 Click on Backup.

3 Click No, unless you first want to check your data.

Whilst Sage Line 50 v8 gives you the option of checking your data before doing a backup, it is advisable to click No and take the backup first, just in case errors are detected and you need copies of the data.

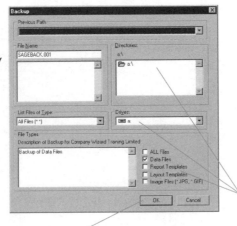

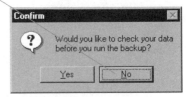

4 To backup to Sage Line 50's default drive, click OK; else, to make changes, follow Steps 5–6.

5 Select required drive, directory and File Types to Backup.

The files you are backing up must have the correct extension to be included in the backup.

6 Click OK, then OK again.

Restoring Data

It is always advisable to run the Check Data option from File, Maintenance after you have restored your data.

Hopefully you should never have to restore your files, but should you be unlucky and suffer data loss or corruption, the Restore procedure allows you to revert to a previous backup. Which backup you restore from is up to you, but it will normally be the most recent.

The Restore facility allows data from your backup disks to replace your old data by erasing it and starting again. It is therefore very important to correctly label disks when you take a backup, and always keep them in a safe place. You may even consider keeping them somewhere other than on the premises in case of fire or theft!

Restoring data will erase the current Sage Line 50 data and replace it with data from your backup disks.

Because the restore procedure erases your old data, any data you entered since the backup is lost and will need entering again. Make sure that the Restore is first necessary, then do the following:

1 From the Sage Line 50 menu, click on File.

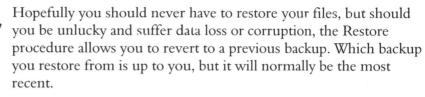

You must restore ALL your data, not just selective data files or a mismatch may exist between the ledger data, causing data corruption.

2 Click on Restore.

If you cancel whilst performing a Restore, Sage requires you to log in again.

3 Click OK to restore data files from default drive, else go to Step 4.

4 If you are restoring from a different drive, select location, here.

5 Click OK to perform the restore.

Changing Global Values

Use the Global Changes option to alter the values for either all or for a selected group of accounts or products.

Certain values in Sage Line 50, such as Credit Limits, have applications throughout the program. From time to time certain record values may need changing for all your records or for a selected group. To save time, these values can be changed quickly and easily by using the Global Changes Wizard. The Wizard guides you with on-screen instructions to make the necessary changes where required.

Values within the customer, supplier and nominal ledger records can be changed as well as certain values within your product records, for example the product sales price could be increased globally by 5% or the re-order level increased for a range of products. To run the Wizard:

Click on the Back button at any time to check what you entered in the previous screen or Cancel to abandon your changes.

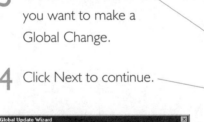

1 From the Sage Line 50 menu, select Tools.

2 Click on Global Changes to start the Wizard.

You can also use the Global Changes Wizard to quickly set up customer turnover and credit limits, supplier turnover and credit limits and nominal budgets.

3 Select the area where you want to make a Global Change.

4 Click Next to continue.

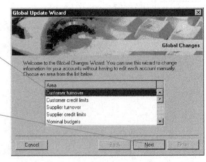

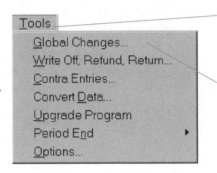

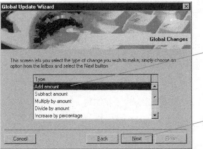

5 Select type of change required.

6 Click Next to continue.

7 You must enter a value here before Sage Line 50 will let you progress.

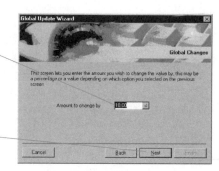

To exit from a wizard at any point, choose the Cancel button or press ALT + F4.

8 Click Next to continue.

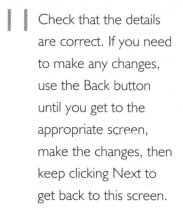

9 Select records required.

10 Click Next to continue.

Use the Global Changes Wizard to quickly set up product sales and purchase prices, Discount Rates, Re-order Levels and Re-order Quantities for your Products.

11 Check that the details are correct. If you need to make any changes, use the Back button until you get to the appropriate screen, make the changes, then keep clicking Next to get back to this screen.

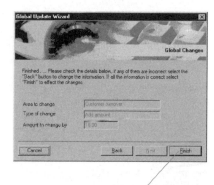

Always check you have entered the correct information as you may not be able to easily undo changes.

12 Click Finish to action the changes.

Whilst the Global Changes Wizard allows you to make changes quickly and easily, be very careful when using it and always double-check your values because when you click Finish, the changes you have entered are immediately actioned. In some cases these are quite major changes, such as increasing all product sales prices by a stated percentage. If you were to accidentally enter the wrong percentage, you cannot easily undo the resulting price changes!

Importing Data

A unit of data in a record can be one of the following data types: Text, e.g. ABcd234, Integer, e.g. 10,20,30,40, Decimal Number, e.g. 25.3,145.05, 0.90.

It can be very laborious entering a lot of data into certain records so Sage Line 50 lets you import data into the following record types – customers, suppliers, products and nominal ledger – provided it conforms to the correct file format. A group of new records can be created and imported directly into Sage Line 50 or existing records updated with new details, replacing records being entering individually.

The text can be produced using any program which allows you to save the file in text format (.txt), for example, a word processing, spreadsheet or accounts package. The text must be in a specific format otherwise it will not be imported correctly and errors will be reported. These files are called CSV files (Comma Separated Values).

The following rules apply:

Avoid import errors by not exceeding maximum data unit length and using the correct data type, e.g., do not enter a decimal number into a integer data unit.

- A comma separates each unit of data, i.e. B01,Bolt,100,0.2

- Each data record takes up a single line.

- Each data record is terminated by pressing ENTER.

- Any spaces at the start or end of a data unit are ignored, but spaces within data units are included.

- Use quotes to include commas within a data unit, i.e. "25, Bell Lane".

- Each data unit in a record must be entered in strict order to avoid being imported incorrectly.

When importing account code data of customers and suppliers records, it is converted to upper-case and restricted to eight characters. Blank spaces are removed.

- Two consecutive commas (,,) will move to the next data unit.

An example of three typical CSV data records:

1,SI,BROWN,4000,2,Supplies,03/10/02,,27.15,T1,Y

2,SC,WHITE,4000,2,Credit,14/10/02,,35.00,T1,N

3,PI,BLACK,5000,4,Equipment,25/11/02,,52.50,T1,Y

To Import a Data File

A SPACE between two commas (, ,) causes the existing data to be erased.

1 From the Sage Line 50 menu, select File.

2 Click Import.

3 Click on correct Import Type here.

Importing a blank unit of data does not overwrite existing data – it leaves it intact and forces a move to the next data unit. Use this feature for changing only selected data in a record.

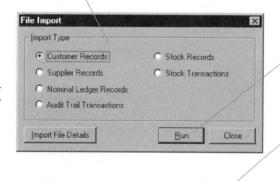

4 Click Run to continue.

5 Select Drive or Directory to Import from.

A list of file import details is available for customer/ supplier records, nominal ledger audit trail transactions, stock records and stock transactions.

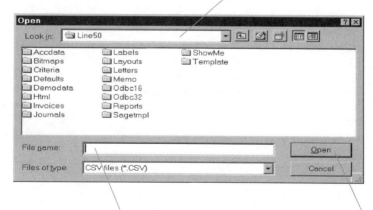

6 Enter Name of File to Import or select from list.

7 Click Open.

File Maintenance

Sage Line 50 v8 provides five important options to manage and check the validity of your data files. These features include checking for input errors, allowing manual data error corrections, data compression, re-indexing and building new data files.

The Check Data option should be used on a daily basis to check for errors, so they can be quickly detected and rectified.

Error Checking

You should use the Check Data facility to check the validity of your data files. If necessary you can then make corrections where required. This facility needs to be run regularly, when making backups and after restoring data.

If there are problems whilst checking the data, a File Maintenance Problem Report dialog box appears which includes a Summary, Comments, Errors or Warnings.

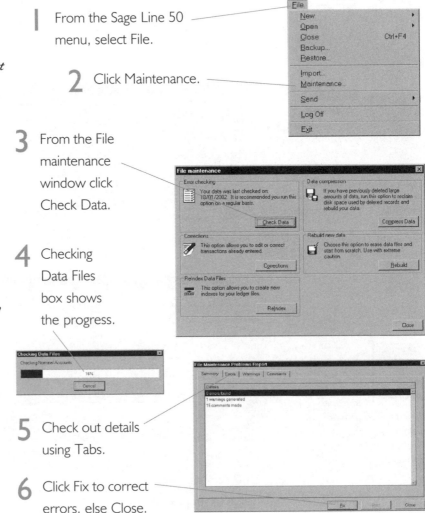

1 From the Sage Line 50 menu, select File.

2 Click Maintenance.

3 From the File maintenance window click Check Data.

4 Checking Data Files box shows the progress.

To print out an error report, select the category tab required from the File Maintenance Problems Report dialog box and click the Print button.

5 Check out details using Tabs.

6 Click Fix to correct errors, else Close.

The reference field can be amended in the Edit Transaction Allocation Record.

Correcting Transactions

Any mistakes made while entering transactions can be corrected using the Corrections option from the File Maintenance window. These transactions, however, can only be edited or deleted if they are still held in the Audit Trail. To correct a transaction:

1 Click Corrections from the File Maintenance window.

Use the Edit button to amend any reference for payments or receipts made against a transaction.

2 Select transaction to correct.

3 Click Edit.

Use the Find button to search for transactions.

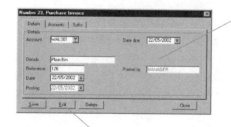

4 For changes to the customer/supplier account, details, reference or date make your corrections here.

5 For more changes click Edit.

Journal entries cannot be amended using the Edit button. To do so select the Journals option from the Nominal Ledger toolbar and make the necessary adjustment by posting a journal entry with the opposite values.

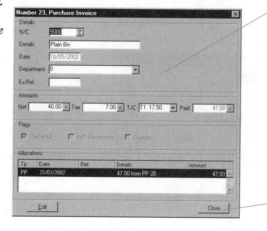

6 To change the nominal account, details, department, amount or VAT amount/code, make your corrections here.

7 Close and Save.

If an amendment cannot be posted, a warning will appear detailing why not.

After confirming a reversal of VAT reconciliation, the Ref entry in the Posting Errors Corrections box reads 'Cancel'.

Make sure you take a back up of your data files BEFORE running Compress Data as the action is irreversible.

Take care when using the Rebuild option as it will clear the contents of your existing data files. USE WITH CAUTION.

New in Sage Line 50 v8, use the ReIndex button to create new indexes for your ledger files should the Check Data option report errors.

Reversing VAT Reconciled Transactions

You can delete a transaction provided it has not been reconciled on the VAT Return. However, any VAT reconciled transaction will display a Reverse button instead of the Delete button in the Transaction Record window. To reverse VAT reconciliation on a transaction:

1 From the Posting Error Corrections window, select transaction and click Edit.

2 To reverse VAT reconciliation click on the Reverse button.

3 Click Yes to confirm.

Data Compression

When there has been a lot of activity, such as deletion or amendments of any records, use the Compress Data option to produce a new set of data files. Sage Line 50 will then reduce file size by removing these deleted records, freeing up disk space. To perform data compression, do this:

1 Click Compress Data from the File Maintenance Box.

2 Click Compress.

3 Click Close.

Rebuild

This Sage Line 50 option is for creating a new or selected set of data files. From the File Maintenance window:

1 Click Rebuild to run option.

2 Select files to rebuild and click OK.

Write Off, Refund and Return

Sage Line 50 procedures for these functions vary depending on whether you are using the Standard VAT Scheme or VAT Cash Accounting. Refer to Help Topics for more information.

Use these options to carry out accounting procedures that affect your customer and supplier accounts, e.g. cheque returns, invoice refunds and outstanding invoice transactions. How you record these depends on your VAT method.

Refunds

Use this facility for credit notes, payments on account and invoices where a money refund is required rather than a replacement of goods or provision of services. If you are using the Standard VAT Scheme, do the following:

1 From the Sage Line 50 menu, click Tools.

2 Click Write Off, Refund, Return...

For VAT Cash Accounting the transaction needs writing off manually.
For more information, refer to Recording Refunds (VAT Cash Accounting) section of the Sage Line 50 Help.

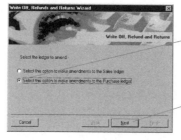

3 Select Ledger required, e.g. Purchase Ledger.

4 Click Next.

5 Select where you want to make the amendments.

6 Click Next.

To find out if you are able to reclaim VAT paid on a Write Off, contact HM Customs & Excise.

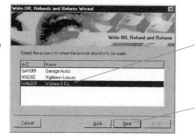

7 Select the account to make the invoice refund to.

8 Click Next to continue.

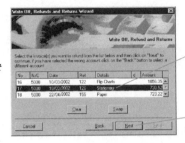

Remember that this option is NOT suitable for anyone using VAT Cash Accounting as it does not adjust the VAT for you.

9 Select the invoice you want to refund.

10 Click Next to continue.

11 Select the bank account you wish to post the journal to.

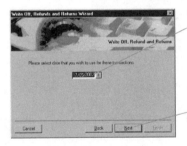

12 Click Next.

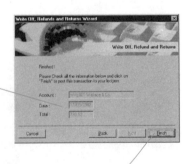

Use the Calendar button to quickly enter your date.

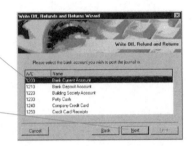

13 Enter the correct date to use for the transaction here.

14 Click Next.

If the presented summary of information is incorrect, use the Back button to return to the appropriate box and modify.

15 The information you have entered is shown in this summary.

16 Check carefully that it is all correct. Use the Back button if you need to make any change, else go to Step 17.

17 Click Finish to post the transaction to your ledgers.

Using a credit note to refund an outstanding customer invoice is known as allocating the credit note to the customer invoice.

Write Off

At times a customer will not or cannot pay an outstanding debt, so the amount can be written off to a bad debt account. The steps are very similar to a Refund, but fewer. Just select the appropriate Write Off for Step 5 (page 165) and follow the simple instructions.

Cheque Returns

Occasionally you may need to record a cheque from a customer that you wish to cancel or that the bank has returned. If you use the Standard VAT Scheme, do this:

When a sales credit note is posted to the customer's account it has the same reference as the refunded invoice.

1 From the Sage Line 50 menu, click Tools.

2 Click Write Off, Refund, Return.

To record a refund using the Write Off, Refund and Return Wizard, the refund must need fully refunding and must not have been removed from the audit trail. If it has been removed or you need to make a partial refund, you must use the manual refund method.

3 Select ledger & click Next.

4 Click Customer Cheque Returns and Next.

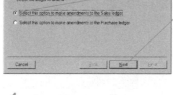

5 Select account, click Next.

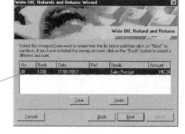

6 Select cheque & carry out Steps 12–17 on Page 166.

Posting Contra Entries

Use the Audit Trail for viewing transactions, as well as Customer and Supplier activity.

Where you have a customer who is also one of your suppliers, you may offset sales invoices against your supplier's purchase invoices. To do this, you use the Contra Entries option from the Tools menu to match one or more sales invoices with your purchase invoices. Sage Line 50 will then automatically update the appropriate ledgers. To post a Contra Entry:

If VAT Cash Accounting is being used, make sure the selected transactions have matching tax codes.

1 From the Sage Line 50 menu, click Tools.

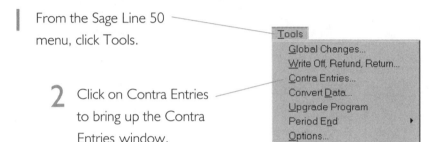

2 Click on Contra Entries to bring up the Contra Entries window.

3 Select Customer (Sales Ledger) and Supplier (Purchase Ledger) accounts.

You cannot amend the values shown in the Total boxes.

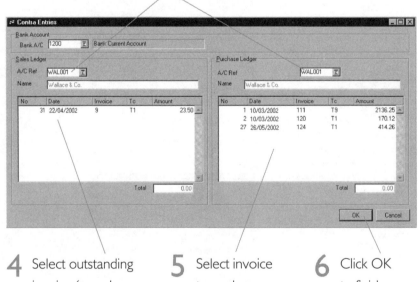

If your totals do not match, a warning message appears asking whether you want to make part-Contra Entries for the lowest amount. If acceptable click the Yes button or No to cancel the Contra Entries.

4 Select outstanding invoice (on sales side) from the list.

5 Select invoice to apply Contra Entry for.

6 Click OK to finish.

Run Period End Functions

If program date needs changing for Month End procedure, select Change Program Date from the Settings menu. Remember to re-set the date back to the correct date.

Period End options are essential monthly and year end procedures for updating the accounting system, for example, for posting accruals, prepayments and depreciation. The Audit Trail can then be cleared of any unwanted transactions whilst stock can be cleared from your Product history if you so wish.

Through running these procedures, you will also be preparing Sage Line 50 so that you are ready to enter transactions for the new financial year.

Month End

At each month end it is important to post your prepayments, accruals and depreciation values. Sage Line 50 will process these transactions automatically and update your nominal account records and audit trail. The option also exists to clear down your month to date turnover figures for your customer and supplier records.

Always Backup your data files before and after Month End procedures.

Once you have run the Month End procedures, this is an opportune time to produce some of your financial reports, for example, the Profit and Loss, Balance Sheet, Trial Balance, Budget and Prior Year Analysis reports. Customer statements and Aged analysis reports for Debtors and Creditors will also prove useful.

Month End Guidelines

Here is a check list for the Month End:

Use File Maintenance Check and Compress Data options to check your files.

1   Check all relevant transactions have been posted.

2   Check recurring entries have been set up and processed.

3   Check prepayments, accruals and depreciation have been set up.

Refer to Sage Line 50 Help system for more information about running Month End procedures.

4   Complete your bank reconciliation.

5   Print product history, valuation and profit reports.

6   Post product journals for your profit and loss and balance sheet.

...cont'd

The month end routine is necessary if you have Prepayments, Accruals, Depreciation, or you wish to clear down the turnover figures for Customers and Suppliers.

Always print off your month end reports for future reference.

New in Sage Line 50 v8, use the Period End button on the Line 50 toolbar to quickly access all your period end functions.

The Year End is an ideal time to remove any fully paid transactions or unwanted records, leaving only outstanding items on your ledgers at the start of the new Financial Year.

If you have multicompany Line 50 you can use the Consolidation option from Period End to merge the data from your separate companies to form one set of financial accounts.

After following the Month End guidelines it is time to run the month end procedure. You will probably want to run it on a day other than the actual last calendar day of the month, as this is often more convenient. You will therefore have to change the program date first. To do this, simply follow these steps:

1 First back up your data files.

2 From the Sage Line 50 menu bar click Settings.

3 Click on Change Program Date.

4 Enter the last day of the month here.

5 Click OK.

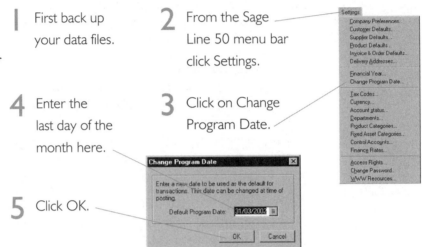

6 From the Sage Line 50 menu, click on Tools.

7 Select Period End.

8 Click on Month End.

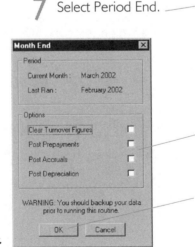

9 Tick the required options.

10 Click OK to run the Month End procedure.

For additional information about running the Year End Procedure and Checklist refer to the Sage Help system.

Year End

Before you run the Year End, Month End procedures must first be completed, together with any final adjustments.

First, when you run Month End on the last month of the current financial year, DO NOT clear the Audit Trail. Once values for the month end have been checked and you are satisfied that they are correct, set the program date to the last date of the current financial year and run Year End:

Take at least two backups of your data files before and after running the Year End routine.

1 Set the program date to the last day of the financial year by doing Steps 1–5 on Page 170.

2 From the Sage Line 50 menu, click on Tools.

Tools
Global Changes...
Write Off, Refund, Return...
Contra Entries...
Convert Data...
Upgrade Program
Period End ▶
Options...

Clear Audit Trail...
Clear Stock...
Month End...
Year End...
Consolidation...

Use File Maintenance to check for errors, correct and compress data files and maximise disk space.

3 Select Period End.

4 Click on Year End.

5 Tick here to update your budget figures for each nominal ledger profit and loss account and each product record with the actual values from the year just ending.

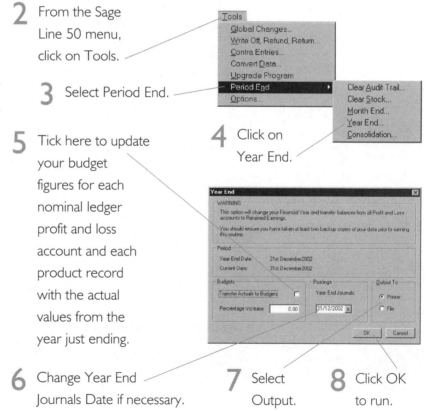

Year End
WARNING
This option will change your Financial Year and transfer balances from all Profit and Loss accounts to Retained Earnings.

You should ensure you have taken at least two backup copies of your data prior to running this routine.

Period
Year End Date: 31st December 2002
Current Date: 31st December 2002

Budgets
Transfer Actuals to Budgets ☐
Percentage Increase   0.00

Postings
Year End Journals
31/12/2002

Output To
⦿ Printer
○ File

OK   Cancel

After Year End check your Financial Year Start Date is correct before entering new transactions.

6 Change Year End Journals Date if necessary.

7 Select Output.

8 Click OK to run.

You must not consolidate companies that have different base currencies.

Lastly, remove any unwanted Customer, Supplier, Nominal, Bank and Product records and reset date. You are now ready to enter transactions for the new financial year.

Clearing the Audit Trail and Stock

Only paid, allocated and reconciled transactions are removed from the Audit Trail.

This option lets you remove paid and reconciled transactions prior to a specified date from the Audit Trail. This makes the ledgers easier to read. Reconciled transactions on the nominal ledger are brought forward as opening balances.

Sage Line 50 can store up to 2,000,000,000 transactions in the Audit Trail, so transactions do not have to be removed, but by deleting unwanted transactions, it will free disk space and provide faster access to information.

The VAT and Bank columns must display the reconciled flag R to be removed from the Audit Trail.

1   From the Tools menu, select Period End and click Clear Audit Trail.

2   Enter required date.

3   Click OK to clear the Audit Trail.

Before running the Clear Stock option, you should back up your data and print your stock valuation and stock history reports. Do likewise before clearing the Audit Trail.

Clear Stock

This option can be run as part of the Month End and Year End procedures. It allows you to decide when to clear transactions from your Product History.

1   From the Tools menu, select Period End and click Clear Stock.

2   Click Yes to continue.

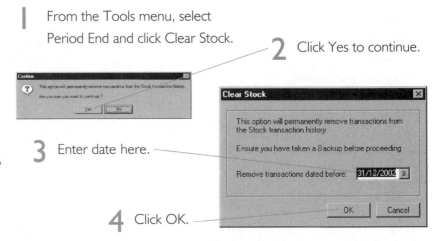

Departmental reporting and activity will be affected by removing transactions from the Audit Trail.

3   Enter date here.

4   Click OK.

The Task Manager

This chapter shows you how to use the Task Manager for setting up useful functions such as a reminder list of tasks to do, i.e., bills to pay, people to contact, etc. It also lets you quickly view the status of your accounts, invoices, sales orders and purchase orders as well as check how much you owe and vice versa.

Covers

Chapter Fifteen

Features of the Tasks Option

Use the Tasks option to set up a list of jobs that you need to do and to prompt you of any tasks that are currently due, overdue or recently completed. By setting up these tasks it acts as a reminder of the actions you need to take to run your business efficiently, produces important information and saves valuable time.

You can use the Tasks option to help you:

Use the Contacts option to check the people you need to speak to, or have spoken with recently, plus any overdue calls that need making. This information is linked directly to the customer and supplier record Contacts tab and will update the relevant future, today, overdue and completed contacts folder.

- Set up a list of tasks that you need to do and also view any tasks that are either completed, due or overdue.

- List people you need to contact today or in the future, or record and view any contacts that you have 'completed' or that are 'overdue'.

- Record the bills you receive and view bills that are paid, due for payment or overdue.

- Check how much you owe your suppliers and, more important, find out how much you are owed by your customers.

From the Company Stack you can view the company information you entered either in the Startup Wizard or in the Company Preferences option from the Sage Line 50 Settings menu.

- Check the account status of your customers and suppliers. For example, you will be able to see at a glance which accounts are over the credit limit, inactive or on-hold.

- View and keep track of any recurring entries you have set up in Sage Line 50.

- Quickly check the status of invoices, sales orders and purchase orders. For example, you may want to see which invoices or credit notes are due for printing or which have yet to be posted.

If you need to clear all your To Do entries in one go simply click on Clear To Do Entries from the Settings menu.

- Keep track of your stock levels. You can easily and quickly check for out of stock items, items which are below re-order level, on order or which have been allocated.

The Task Manager Desktop

The Application toolbar offers different options with different functions, depending upon the Tasks chosen from the Stacked toolbar.

Your Sage Line 50 Task Manager desktop features a menu bar, a stacked toolbar, an application toolbar and a split screen, with tree view on the left and list view on the right.

From the desktop you can set up tasks, remind yourself of jobs to do etc. To bring up the desktop do the following:

1 From the Sage Line 50 toolbar, click on the Tasks button.

2 The Menu Bar provides a list of options using drop-down menus.

3 The stacked toolbar area.

4 List View area.

Options available from the Application toolbar are also available from the Tasks menu. These include New, Open, Delete, Pay and Properties.

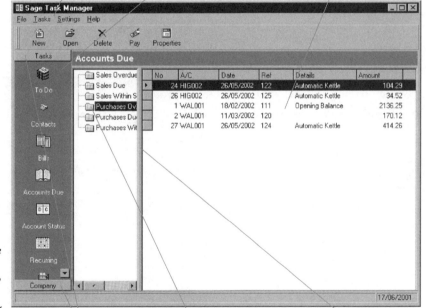

Use the List View screen (right hand side of the screen) as a shortcut to your tasks, transactions, bills, recurring entries etc. by simply double-clicking on the required entry.

5 Click on the Tasks or Company buttons for the respective toolbars.

6 Select a folder in the Tree View area to bring up a list.

7 Resize the View areas by dragging from here.

Setting Up a To Do Task

Use the shortcut key CTRL+N, or click the right hand mouse button and select New from the pop-up menu to set up a new To Do task.

Use the To Do option to create a list of tasks you need to complete. The type of tasks include a General Reminder, Send overdue letters, Print management reports etc. Any additional information that may prove useful can be entered within the Description and Notes boxes.

Once saved, the task appears in the Current Tasks folder on the To Do list. This list can then be viewed at any time. To set up a To Do task, proceed as follows:

1 From the Task Manager, click on the To Do option from the Tasks stacked toolbar.

2 Click New from the application toolbar.

If the Task Complete box is selected, the task is moved from the Current Tasks or Overdue Tasks list to the Complete Tasks list.

4 Enter date when task is due for completion.

3 Select the reminder type from the drop down list box.

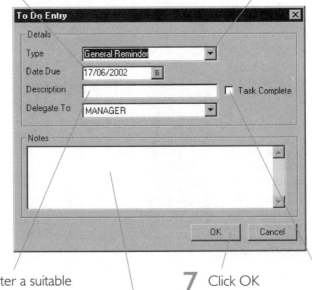

When you save your task it appears in the Current Tasks folder on the To Do List.

To delete a task, highlight it from the Current, Overdue, or Completed Tasks and click Delete from the File menu.

5 Enter a suitable Description, e.g., chase overdue payments.

6 Type any special instructions here.

7 Click OK to save.

8 Check here when complete.

Recording a New Bill

When the bill details are saved, it will appear in the Current Bills folder on the Bills list. If required you can edit your bill details.

The Bills option provides a useful and convenient way of recording all your bills, such as rates, rent, etc. Once the payment information is entered and saved, the bill will appear in the Current Bills folder on the Bills list. These details can be edited if required at this stage.

Use the Task Manager then to quickly view which bills are paid, due or overdue. To record a new bill:

1 Using Task Manager, click on the Bills option from the Tasks stacked toolbar.

2 Click New from the File menu.

Once the Bills option has been selected from the Tasks stacked toolbar, you can use the shortcut key CTRL+N to record a new bill.

3 Enter the nominal code for paying the bill to, e.g., if paying your telephone bill the default nominal ledger account is 7502.

4 Describe your transaction here.

References entered into the Ref box will appear in the Audit Trail for cross referencing purposes.

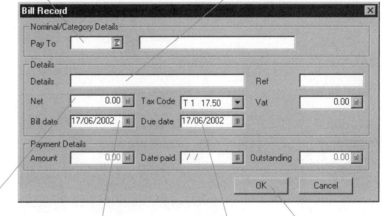

If a bill is not paid by the Due Date entered, the task is moved to the Overdue Bills folder.

5 Enter Net amount of the bill here.

6 Enter date bill received.

7 Enter date bill is due to be paid.

8 Check all Details and click OK to save.

Paying a Bill

Use the Pay option to quickly and easily pay any current/outstanding bills which have been previously set up using Task Manager. To action bill payment the only detail required is the Bank Account nominal code you want to pay the bill from, as follows:

After paying a selected bill, it is moved from the Current Bills or Overdue Bills folder to the Paid Bills folder. The bill payment details are updated on the Bill Record.

1 Select Bills from the Tasks stacked toolbar.

3 Select the bill required from the List View.

2 Select either Current Bills or Overdue Bills folder from the Tree view.

4 Click the Pay option from the application toolbar.

An alternative way to pay a bill is by selecting the Pay option from the Application toolbar.

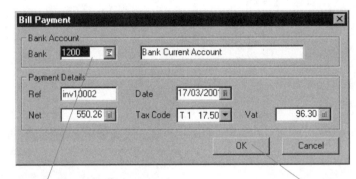

5 Enter nominal code of Bank account to pay the bill from.

6 Click OK to pay the bill.

To print the activity on a certain nominal account just click Nominal, then Reports in Line 50 and select the Nominal Activity report layout.

7 The bill is now paid and moves into the Paid Bills folder.

8 Click on the Paid Bills folder and double-click on the bill you have just paid.

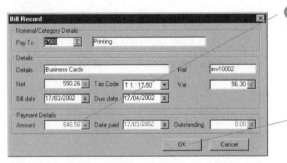

9 Note the Bill Record is updated to show payment details.

10 Click OK to close.

Accounts Due

To view more details about a transaction, select the transaction and use shortcut key ALT+ENTER.

Use the Account Due option from the Tasks stack to identify who owes you money, i.e., Sales Overdue, Sales Due and Sales Within Settlement. You can also check who you owe money to by viewing the Purchases Overdue, Purchases Due and Purchases Within Settlement folders.

To find out which customers owe you money

1 From the Tasks stacked toolbar, select Accounts Due and click the Sales Overdue folder.

2 Note transaction list of overdue payments.

Use the Phone button to automatically dial your customer telephone number. Your computer (with modem) needs to share the same line as your telephone.

3 For more details, select a transaction.

4 Click Properties from the application toolbar.

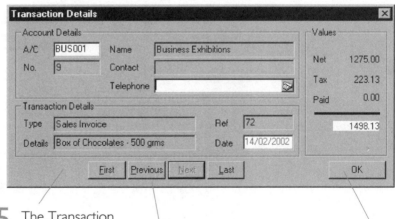

To view details of different transactions on the list, click the First, Previous, Next or Last buttons.

5 The Transaction Details window appears.

7 When finished click OK.

For a printout of debtors refer to the Customers Reports window.

6 Use these buttons to move between different transactions in the list.

Account Status

The Account Status option lets you view accounts that match certain criteria, for example, Sales Over Credit Limit, Sales On Hold, Purchase Over Credit Limit or Purchase On Hold. If you require more detailed information about a transaction, select it and click the Properties button from the application toolbar.

Use the shortcut key ALT+ENTER to view transaction properties.

1 From the Line 50 Task Manager window, choose the Account Status option from the Tasks stacked toolbar.

In the Account Details window use the First, Previous, Next and Last buttons to move between different account transactions.

2 Select the folder you require from the Tree View list.

3 Highlight the required account from the List view.

Use the telephone button to let Sage Line 50 dial a customer for you when you want to speak to them about their account.

4 Click the Properties button on the application toolbar.

You can print out a list of customers On Hold or customers Over Credit Limit from the Sage Line 50 Customers, Reports window.

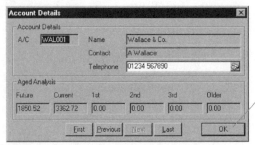

5 When finished, click OK to exit.

The Recurring Option

To set up recurring entries, select the Recurring option from the Bank toolbar.

Using the Task Manager you can view any recurring entries you have set for various transaction types, namely Receipt, Payment, Journal Debit or Journal Credit.

You can view the individual details about the transactions, but you cannot change these details. To view details about a recurring payment you set up in Sage Line 50, do the following:

You cannot change your recurring entry details from within the Task Manager.

1 From the Line 50 Task Manager window, choose the Recurring option from the Tasks stacked toolbar.

2 Select the folder you require from the Tree View list, e.g., Payments.

3 Highlight the required payment from the List view.

4 Click the Properties button on the application toolbar.

For detailed information about recurring entries, select transaction and choose the Properties option from the application toolbar.

5 The details appear for the selected recurring entry.

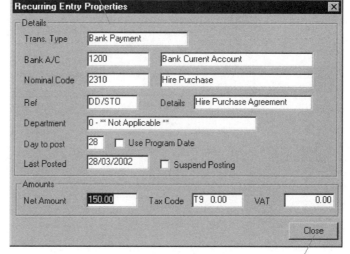

Save time with Version 7 & 8 by processing a recurring entry at any time during the month.

6 Click Close when finished.

Stock Option

The Task Manager is a handy way of keeping track of your stock. It provides you with a fast and efficient way of seeing what is out of stock, below the reorder level, on order and allocated.

By using Task Manager for regular monitoring of stock you can make decisions about items which need re-ordering or stock you are waiting for.

Stock transactions are for viewing only; a properties facility is not available.

Sage Line 50 can only provide accurate reporting and stock tracking if the correct information has been entered in the first place. Plan to make full use of Sage Line 50's extensive stock details recording facilities.

Use the horizontal and vertical scroll bars to view all transaction details.

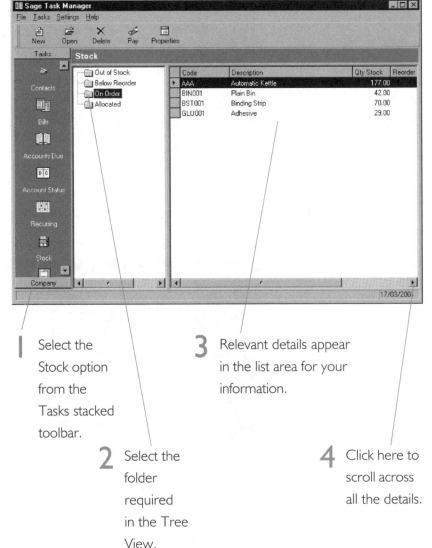

1 Select the Stock option from the Tasks stacked toolbar.

2 Select the folder required in the Tree View.

3 Relevant details appear in the list area for your information.

4 Click here to scroll across all the details.

Invoices Option

An alternative way to view your invoices is to select Tasks from the Task Manager menu bar and click Invoices.

Within Task Manager you can view the status of any invoices or credit notes that you have recorded.

Invoices and credit notes are listed separately depending on whether they have been printed or posted. You can also quickly view which invoices or credit notes need printing or posting.

For example, do the following to quickly view a list of invoices which you have not yet printed:

1 From the Task Manager window, click on the down button on the Tasks stacked toolbar until Invoices appears.

To print/post an invoice or credit note or record an invoice/credit note number, return to the Invoicing option on the Sage Line 50 toolbar then select your transaction and use the Print option.

2 Click on the Invoices option.

3 Select Inv to Print folder.

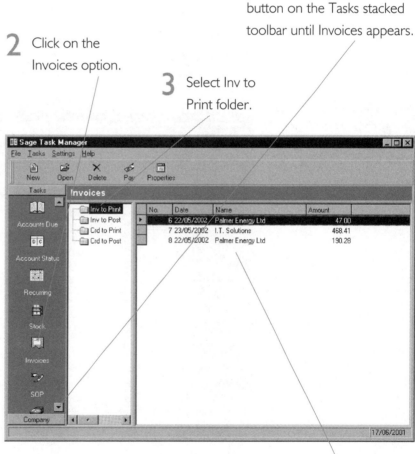

Properties function is not available when viewing invoices or credit notes in the Task Manager.

4 A list of invoices not yet printed appears.

Sales Order Processing

You can also access Sales Orders by selecting Tasks from the Task Manager menu and clicking Sales Orders.

From Task Manager you can view the status of your Sales Orders directly. A selection of folders is available for you to view the type of sales orders required, for example, orders that are 'To Allocate', 'Cancelled', 'Held', etc.

(It is important to remember, however, that you can only view the details in this screen. If you need to create a new Sales Order or make any changes, you will have to return to the SOP option in Sage Line 50).

As an example, if you wanted a list of completed Sales Orders, you could use the SOP Reports facility to print out a suitable report, or you can do a quick view from the Task Manager as follows:

I From Task Manager, click the SOP option on the Tasks Stacked toolbar.

2 Select the Completed folder.

You will need to return to the SOP option on the Sage Line 50 toolbar to perform any sales order functions.

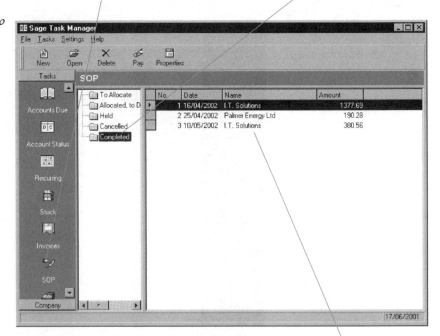

3 A list of Completed Sales Orders appears in the View area.

Purchase Order Processing

Just as with Sales Orders, use the Task Manager to quickly display the status of your Purchase Orders when you do not need a printed copy. Options available are To Order and To Deliver.

For example, to view a list of Purchase Orders that are 'To Deliver' follow these simple steps:

To access Purchase Orders from the Task Manager menu, select Tasks and click Purchase Orders.

1 From the Task Manager window, choose the POP option from the Tasks stacked toolbar (you may have to use the down button on the stacked toolbar to bring it into view).

2 Select the To Deliver folder in the Tree View.

You cannot alter transaction details using this Task Manager facility. You will need to return to the POP option on the Sage Line 50 toolbar to perform any purchase order functions.

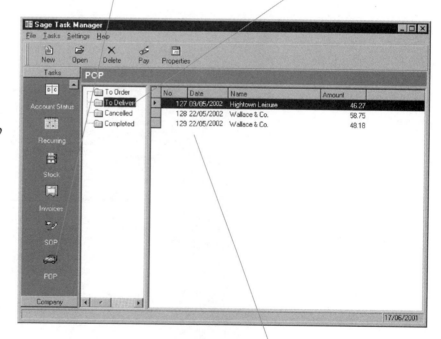

3 A list of Purchase Orders To Deliver appears in the View area.

The Company Stack

This feature is useful for quickly viewing your Company Details, such as Name, Address, Telephone, Fax, VAT Reg. No., Web Site and E-mail.

You can also select Company Details from the Settings menu on the Line 50 Task Manager toolbar to view or amend your Company Details.

These details, however, cannot be edited using this screen. To do so you will need to exit from the Task Manager and return to Sage Line 50. Then, select Company Preferences from the Sage Line 50 Settings menu and make your changes using the Address tab (see page 11).

To quickly view Company Details from the Task Manager just do the following:

1 Click on the Company button at the foot of the stacked toolbar.

2 Click on Company Details to view information.

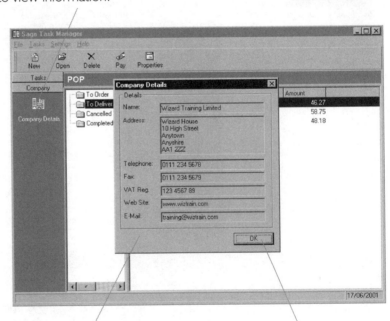

3 The Details window appears.

4 Click OK to close.

Index

D

E

F

G

H

I

J

L

M

N

O

P

Q

R

S